MARKETING
with Social Media

BILL BELEW, PHD

Cover and interior images illustrated by Benjamin Belew. Reprinted with permission.

www.kendallhunt.com
Send all inquiries to:
4050 Westmark Drive
Dubuque, IA 52004-1840

ISBN 978-1-4652-3921-1

Printed in the United States of America
10 9 8 7 6 5 4 3 2 1

Contents

Preface   iv

CHAPTER 1   Why Me, Lord?   1

CHAPTER 2   Blog—What's in a Name?   7

CHAPTER 3   5 Reasons Why Business Blogs Are King of Social Media   11

CHAPTER 4   4 Keys to Get Serious Traffic to Your Web Site   21

CHAPTER 5   5 Biggest Obstacles to Getting Your Blog Started and What to Do to Overcome Them   30

CHAPTER 6   10 Things to Consider When Starting a Blog   36

CHAPTER 7   22 Reasons Why You Might Want to Blog   42

CHAPTER 8   21 Characteristics That Define Quality in a Blog   57

CHAPTER 9   How Much and How Long?   72

Conclusion - It's Not Easy, It's Not Hard   76

Epilogue   77

Glossary   81

Preface

There are a lot of different kinds of people who can benefit from what they will learn in this book.

Business people - established businesses, startups, entrepreneurs. Every business has or absolutely should have an online presence. And every business I know would like to have more customers, clients or leads. Gosh, even Toyota would like more customers. This book will teach you how to get more people to walk through you door, both virtually and physically. This is called getting people into the sales funnel.

Students - business, journalism, artists, vocational. Everybody has something to sell. Themselves (not like that), their service, their product, their skill. This book will teach you how to get noticed, to be considered a thought leader, to earn respect in your field.

Hobbyists - knitters, climbers, cooks, pet owners, coffee drinkers. All of you will learn in this book how you can get more traffic to your web site and make money by writing about your hobby. Enough money to feed your hobby and then some.

Writers - novelists, poets, photographers. If I had a nickel for every person I have met just in the past few years who has written a book and is looking for readers = read sales of their books, I'd be rich. They are writers looking for readers. I have readers waiting for me to write a book. In this book you will learn how to get readers for your book.

Bloggers - social media experts. Make no mistake. Business blogging is still King of social media. In this book you will learn what it takes to make your blog stand out. There are 10s of millions of blogs. Some have to be good. Why not yours? In this book you will learn what good is when it comes to blogging. Other so-called social media experts are all working diligently to get fans, friends and followers to their web site. You had better have something worth coming to. This book will teach you how.

You - the visibility seeker. You have picked up this book because you want more visibility. Or perhaps someone gave you this book because they think you are the kind or person who has something to offer if you could just get the word out. I just moments ago had a conversation with an older woman who was booted out of her Silicon Valley engineering job and is now falling back on her first love. Drawing - hand and digital. She's quite good if you like her style. But nobody knows about her. This book can teach her how to get the word out on her skills.

If you don't want more visibility then this book is not for you. Save your time and stop reading now. Give the book to someone else perhaps. If you do want more visibility, you have come to the right place.

CHAPTER 1 — Why Me, Lord?

In 1971, Kris Kristofferson was 35 and I was in my senior year of high school. The third single on his fourth album (same as the title to this chapter) salvaged an otherwise mediocre (my opinion, of course) collection of songs. I can remember singing along with KK in my '61 VW bug. Did you know that VW bugs that year did NOT have gas gauges? You just drove them till they ran out of gas, then flipped a lever next to the driver's seat that opened up a reserve tank that was good for about 10 miles. After that it was push. I point this out because it is in my nature to not know how far or what my limits are. I just go till I run out of gas. Then I reach for a bit of reserve and hope I can make it to someplace soon enough to be refilled.

Forty years later and Kris is still singing that song. Me, I am humming the tune and wondering out loud, too, "Why me, Lord, what have I ever done?" to be able to write a book on how to get readers to a blog or a web site. I have an answer to that question.

I made the leap to professional blogger in March 2006. I started with zero readers a day, no blog posts in the archives, and no love. By no love I mean nobody knew I was blogging, nobody was linking to me. I can remember the first time someone showed up, the first comment, the first time someone yelled at me (yelling is more common than praise!), even the first time I got comment spam. Yay! Comment spam, by the way, is not a bad thing for a while. Reason being is that if you ain't getting comment spam you ain't nobody. In other words, if the spammers can't find your blog, neither can the search engines or anybody else for that matter. Unless, of course, you send your friend or your mom a direct link where they can find you.

Before making the leap to wanting to make a living at blogging I played around at a free blog host site for a share of the revenues. I never did make any money there. Or maybe the guy just never followed through on his end. The site has been removed and all the content I created there is gone now. I didn't see much future in blogging. But I met a guy through that network who told me he was writing for a separate business network. He encouraged me to apply. I checked it out and soon learned that business network did not have anything in their network related to international business. (I had lived in Asia for nearly 20 years, mostly Japan, but also spent significant time in China, Far East Russia, and India.) And I had confidence to write about doing business in Asia and the goings on that affected business there. I proposed a topic to the powers that be and it was accepted. www.panasianbiz.com (affectionately called PAB) was born. The blog was all about business in the Pan Asian region, and the network paid me by the post. Blog, blog, blog and even more blogging, and little by little readers began to trickle in. I remember when I was excited to get 100 unique visitors in a month! Then 100 in a day. We (my wife and I) celebrated, bought ice cream, baked cookies, shared milestones with friends, and I got ridiculed by those same friends. Mostly it was good-natured ribbing, but not really. I am convinced that they thought I was crazy. "Make a living blogging? Good luck with that." But I kept on writing.

Then PAB gave birth to www.risingsunofnihon.com (all about Japan) and www.zhonghuarising .com (all about China). I proposed to the network owners that I write about the business of for-profit education. Accepted!

www.thebizofknowledge.com came into the blogosphere. I wrote like a mad dog on the kitchen table every morning in our small condominium in Campbell, CA. My, um, office smelled like a Chinese kitchen. Mostly because I was writing in the kitchen next to my Chinese mother-in-law who was always cooking up something. The place was 800 square feet, we had one bath, and as I mentioned, my in-laws were staying with us. After finishing my self-assigned writing quota each morning, I made for a local college where I taught general education classes: writing, math, psychology, environmental science, public speaking.

I had four sites going. The network owners gave the writers, me included, an upper limit on how many posts we could write each month. And I hit the limit every month . . . every, every month. I wrote 15 posts of 200 + words each and every day . . . every, every day. (Praise God for schedulers so I didn't have to publish every day. The publishing tool did that for me.) And thank God for the upper limit. I no doubt would have written even more had I not been told to stop. In retrospect, 150 articles/site/month is a good pace. I will explain later in this book. Three of these sites eventually grew to more than 1 million unique visitors EACH. The one that didn't was handed off to another writer who eventually abandoned the site. PAB has over 25 million views (Winter 2012). Much of that is on China and Japan. But these days most of it is on India.

The blogosphere, however, does not always run smoothly. You would think—write, hit publish, rinse, repeat. What could go wrong? Plenty is the answer.

There were some hard times to be sure, not to mention when the blog network I was part of fell out of love with a search engine they were hugely dependent on and lost almost ALL of its search traffic. This one search engine can account for about two-thirds of all traffic that a site gets. Like 'em or love 'em, bloggers who try to make money with their sites work for search engines. I could say, "I work for Google or Bing or Yahoo or Baidu or Yandex or Blekko or Dogpile or. . . ." But that topic is beyond the scope of this book. When the network lost its search engine love, they had to lay off their writers. I bought my sites and content that I had maintained for them and went off on my own to create my own mini-network of sites.

In the six -plus years I have been blogging our monthly average income has been enough to pay our sizable monthly Silicon Valley mortgage payments. I had to save up from previous months at times and borrow from coming months at others, but we have a home in Sunnyvale, CA about two miles from Yahoo, three from Google, and two-ish from Apple, among other tech giants. (You would think any one of these three giants could leak enough of their combined $10 billion quarterly profits my way to buy me a house. Not happening.) For a long time, blogging was the primary source of income for my wife, daughter and me. My wife has since gotten a job and now out-earns me. Good for me, for us.

I have written more than 12,000 articles, all of them around 200 words each, sometimes more but not usually less. I have since hired writers and acted as editor. After which I hired an editor and now just spot check what goes on at my sites. But I wrote those first 12,000 articles myself. I laid the foundation of my sites.

In April of 2011 my sites got more than 100,000 page views in one day for the first time. It was really cool. We danced, literally, and hooted and hollered. But what is cooler than that is that from April to December of 2012 my sites have been averaging 115K page views EVERY day. We are not working harder. We are writing the same number of articles on the same topics but the traffic is growing. It grows just because more people are coming online. This is real organic growth. I have had more than 597,000 page views in one day. More than 65,000 people have come in less than an hour! 10,000 views in a minute. That's 166 visitors per second!

That much traffic can be quite intoxicating, to be honest, not to mention addictive. It is easy (not right, but easy) for bloggers to find self-worth in how much traffic they get, or feel low self-esteem if they don't get very much. I have an Excel spreadsheet of how many views my sites have had each and every day for the last 2,000 and some-odd days. At one point I was keeping a record by morning, afternoon, evening, and night. Lots and lots of numbers. Lots of wasted time. **But now I KNOW how many readers I can get if I follow a few guidelines and post a certain number of posts at a certain word count in the right format over a certain length of time. I KNOW from experience—call it empirical data—what it takes.** And I share that knowledge with you here.

I have taken 10 different and unrelated topics to more than 1,000,000 unique visitors EACH. A visitor or unique visitor is how many people show up at a site. A page view is how many pages are viewed at a site after the visitors come. I am talking about visitors. I am not talking about hits. This is how many people actually opened up my site. The page view total is about 1.5–2.2 times the number of visitors I have received . . . depending on the topic. A good page view to unique visitor ratio is a good indicator of the quality of a site. A high ratio shows that readers like what they found enough so that they turned the pages to look at other stuff on the site. A ratio or 1:5 or better is a good ratio.

If I got 1,000,000 people to show up at one site, the your could reasonably surmise that I was lucky. And you may be right in thinking so. If I got that many readers twice, then perhaps I am really lucky. Three times—really, really, lucky. Four times—really, really, really lucky. But 10 times? It's not luck anymore. To be honest, I am a lucky person. Except that all my luck is bad. **I know the formula for getting good legitimate traffic to your site regardless of the niche . . . well almost.** The legitimate, hard, slow, but long-lasting formula.

The topics my sites cover are China, India, Japan, Environment, Christian Worldview, Bollywood, Cricket, News Headlines, South Asia, and Blogging and Blogosphere.

Following are a few screen captures taken from some of my sitemeters to give you confidence in believing that what I am saying is indeed true. Please don't just take my word for it. Take a look and know, feel in your bones, that what I am telling you is true and that what I teach will work for you IF you work.

CosmoFairNetworks Site Summary	
VISITS	
Total	20,026,283
Average Per Day	12,623
Average Visit Length	0:45
Last Hour	698
Today	14,561
This Week	88,359
PAGE VIEWS	
Total	27,781,675
Average Per Day	21,605
Average Per Visit	1.7
Last Hour	1,054
Today	22,583

CosmoFairNetworks Combined Views

PanAsianBiz Site Summary	
VISITS	
Total	14,042,680
Average Per Day	15,285
Average Visit Length	1:12
Last Hour	360
Today	132
This Week	106,994
PAGE VIEWS	
Total	21,269,811
Average Per Day	21,654
Average Per Visit	1.4
Last Hour	491
Today	200

PanAsian

FilmyFair Site Summary	
VISITS	
Total	2,873,478
Average Per Day	2,250
Average Visit Length	1:49
Last Hour	123
Today	165
This Week	15,750
PAGE VIEWS	
Total	4,143,754
Average Per Day	4,506
Average Per Visit	2.0
Last Hour	206

Celebrity

Greenpacks.org
Site Summary

VISITS

Total	2,785,790
Average Per Day	3,428
Average Visit Length	0:44
Last Hour	133
Today	2,613
This Week	23,998

PAGE VIEWS

Total	3,620,102
Average Per Day	4,711
Average Per Visit	1.4
Last Hour	180
Today	3,478

Environment

Bill Belew
Examiner since March 1, 2009 | 1 | Edit profile

What I Examine: Christian Worldview, International Sports, India Headlines, Blogosphere Buzz, Smartphones, Blogging

REPORTING   ACTIVITIES   FAVORITES   SUBSCRIPTIONS

Reporting

View:

India Headlines Examiner

This year at a glance   View: Current Year

Your pageviews	National Average
6,066,990	7,535

India Headline News

A writer friend of mine attended a recent workshop of mine. We met again in a weekly critique group, and she told me that she had attended another similar workshop to mine held by another guy here in the Valley. "He said pretty much the same kind of stuff," she told me. Hmm . . .

I looked the speaker up—Peter Muffleslopper (not his real name). His site gets less than 50 visits a day, IF that many. Indeed, he may know how to get traffic to a web site, but he hasn't done it himself. Another friend of mine, Jackson (not his real name, either), knows how to rock climb, do origami, and quilt because he learned how in a book he had read. But he can't physically do those things. He just knows how.

I not only know how to get traffic, I have done it, and I continue to do it. There is an old saying, "Those who can, do. Those who can't teach." What about those who can do it, have done it and can teach others how to do it? They are experts. That's me. I can do it and I want you, the reader, to have confidence when you read what I write here that it has worked and will work for you. This book is not a theory on how you might get results if you follow certain steps. It's a **report** on how results were achieved by following certain steps, again and again, and again and again and again and again, and again and again.

I have been an educator nearly all my adult working life. Besides teaching university in Japan, I also taught graduate school in upstate New York and did dissertation advising for PhD students for the world's largest online accredited university. In one of my classes I laid out the pros and cons of the evolution versus creation debate. Apparently I had done a pretty effective job of presenting both sides of this debate. So much so that one of my best students, exasperated, jumped up, pounded the table, and said, "Mr. Belew, just tell us the answer." There is a lot of what works, what might work, what is best, and what may or may not be the best method to get good relevant organic search engine results to your web site. It is not my intention to confuse you or even to give you a lot to think about. I do not intend to write a long book just because I can or even try to impress you with all my, um, deep knowledge. I will give you answers. I will tell you what works and what worked for me over and over again. The principles laid out in this book will work regardless of algorithm changes and the pop up or disappearance of some new social medium. In time, I may write a book that explains the whys and wherefores. But not here. Like Nike might say, "Just do it." In this book is what works.

And for those who care, I did NOT dress "the King." That's important to me because yet another writer's critique group wouldn't let me participate in their writer's critique group because they thought I had some connection to Elvis. Bill Belew (same name, same spelling, but no relation to me) was the costume designer for the King. I don't even wish I were him. That Bill Belew is dead. I am very much alive . . . living life and living it to the full. When that Bill Belew died, a bunch of friends came to my site asking, "Bill, are you all right?" I enjoyed the traffic but it wasn't fun to know that it was at the expense of someone else.

With no sense of false modesty, honest to goodness, I do not consider myself a good writer. I know some good writers. I am not one of them. I know how to write. I can spell and punctuate and deduct points from my students who can't. But I cannot write particularly well. I spent some 20 years in Far East Asia. I went days, weeks without speaking a word of English. Indeed, there's a big hole in my English writing and speaking ability. I can read but I often don't have the confidence in my word choice nor do I have the facility with words to make sentences flow and ooze clarity and tickle ears and . . . see, I can't do it. What I can do is write stuff that gets read. I know how to do that. What I do know is how to balance an article between appeal to a reader and appeal to the search engine. If you write only with a reader in mind, a search engine won't find you. If you write only for search engines, readers will find you but they won't stay around. There's an ideal balance between appeal to readers (first) and search engines (second). Another word for ideal is optimal or optimized. When you are able to write content that appeals to real people and can be found by the search engines you have search engine optimization. And that's what I know how to do. That's what bloggers want—people to find and come to their web sites and enjoy being there. People come to my web sites. In this book I will tell you how to bring people to your web site, too.

Test: Fill in the blank—If Bill Belew can do this and he doesn't write all that well, then _____ can do it, too! Answer is below.

Answer to test question: "I"

CHAPTER 2   Blog—What's in a Name?

The way I see it, the main problem with blogs is what they are called—blogs. What an ugly name. *Blog* sounds too much like blah__g, blah__g, blah___g. And unfortunately too many folks think that is what is going on at blogs: Bloggers are just blah-blah-blahging away about their love life or lack of, their job or lack of, their rants and the like. Even more unfortunately, that is exaclty what some bloggers are doing. It's okay for them. But it's not oaky to put me in the same category.

Not me. Nope. Uh-uh.

When people ask me what I do for a living, I sometimes just for fun tell them I own a network of dynamic web sites with interactive capability. Dynamic because they are updated often, even multiple times daily; and interactive because readers can comment and give feedback to the author and to each other.

To which I get, "Ooo . . ." "Whoa!" or "Cool." But more often than not a blank stare and "Huh?" To that last group I explain, "I own a blog network." At which point they roll their eyes and think so loudly I can hear the thought bubble pop, "The guy [me] has no love life, no job, and just gripes a lot online because he has nothing else to do." Also not so. I do have a love life (I don't write about that as it's really no one else's business), and a job, and I am definitely not a griper.

A turn of the century cowboy philosopher, Will Rogers, cured me of complaining with one of his nuggets of wisdom. He said something like, "I used to complain about not having any shoes until one day I saw a man with no feet." I do NOT complain in my blogs or in real life, and I don't particularly care to read when others whine either. Besides, blogging can be a lot of good things. Blogs can provide information. They can act as a forum. They can be a creative outlet, the first steps in writing a book, building a platform, gaining an audience. Well-trafficked blogs can also produce income. As I said before, revenue from my blogs pays my sizable Silicon Valley mortgage. Let me put it this way. While my wife, daughter and I are watching a movie at the theater, my web sites will make more money than it costs us to be there. And that is just from advertisements placed on my sites. That does not include book sales, consulting, workshops and the like.

This book is about how to create a successful business blog. Success, of course, is relative. Some bloggers might measure it by how many people showed up at their site today, yesterday, this month, or this year. Some preachers I know (okay, all the preachers I know) rightly or wrongly measure success by how many people show up in church on Sundays. People who say numbers aren't important or numbers are not a good way to measure value usually don't have any numbers. Indeed numbers are not the only way to measure worth or progress. They are, however, a quantifiable way of determining effectiveness.

Others might determine success by the number of books they sell to visitors from their sites, and still others will be happy about an increase in comments they get and the difference they are making in the lives of their readers.

Finally, some will be happy to just be writing publicly or getting the word out on something they are very passionate about: a mission, a charity, an event, a rite of passage.

I measure success at my blogs by a combination of all the above. But mostly I just use the metrics of how many people (unique visitors) showed up, how many pages (page views) they turned, how long (time on site) they stayed at my site, and whether or not they just bounced off (bounce rate).

In this book, my simple goal is to tell you, the reader, by the numbers, from my experience, my personal case studies as well as some of the case studies of folks who have followed my advice (as opposed to theory), what it takes to get good, relevant, free, organic, search engine results. A LOT of results. I will teach you how to get as many as 1 million visitors or more to your blog. (As of this writing—winter 2012—I have well over 100 million views. Seriously!) For those aiming a little lower and hoping for results a bit quicker or more local, I can teach you, too, how to get a thousand or so visitors to your blogs EACH day. What you the reader/blogger do for or with those visitors once they show up—show them ads, teach them something, entertain them, convert them, or just use the blog site as a very findable platform for anything else you have to offer—is, of course, up to you.

After giving reasons (I feel like the apostle Paul, "let the reader understand") why I have the authority to teach you how to be successful with your blogs, I will address eight key points:

1. Why blogs are king of social media
2. Keys to get serious traffic to your web site
3. Obstacles and solutions to get your blog started
4. Why anyone would want to blog
5. What makes a good blogger
6. What makes a quality blog
7. How much effort it takes to build a successful blog
8. How long it takes to build a blog readership of thousands daily

At various points you will see "for example" or some similar expression. WARNING: I am likely to wander off into a personal anecdote, a story about one of my kids, or even a Bible story of some sort. I am a Christian and I do not apologize for being so. Applying Christian principles to the blogosphere has brought my blogs and me to where they are. And I do like to tell stories. So, feel free to skip the anecdotes, although they will help illustrate some key points and if nothing else let you know more about me.

It is my sincere desire that what you learn in this book, applied faithfully to your blogs, indeed makes a difference in your blogging life and in your life in general, not to mention in the lives of your readers.

Here is a long list of comments I received anonymously on feedback forms or via the comment function on my blog—in no particular order.

"I met Bill in 2007. We were both living our dream of getting food on our tables through writing. He was doing it exceptionally great and I had a lot to learn from him. That's because he knows a lot about driving traffic to a website, be it an already established website or a new one. In all honesty, Bill knows stuff!" *Bucharest, Romania*

"Excellent presentation: Presenter's style + generous information are appreciated. Great coverage w/ direct answers, humor & stories. The actual demo during Q & A was most helpful. Thank you." *Santa Clara, CA*

"The presentation was fabulous. Bill was engaging, interesting and passionate. I learned a ton and look forward to hearing more." *Monterey, CA*

"Bill Belew has mastered: 'how to bring sustainable 1Mil + monthly visitors to your blog & make a living.' Though we've been running blogs for years, in only short two meetings Bill has helped us in transforming our blog; where to some of his pointers we've said 'Wow, that's incredible . . .' In the space of only a couple of months, our blog traffic has doubled and our ad-sense earning became more than 2x. Trust me, Bill Belew is who you need if you want to make your blog go from zero to hero." *eBay*

"Thank you for the very useful handouts. Great! Great information. Thank you." *Cupertino, CA*

"When I met Bill Belew I could barely spell BLOG, but with his help my blog has gone from a vague dream to one of the top 1% of blogs world-wide. I cannot recommend Bill highly enough for technical and inspirational guidance." *Fremont, CA*

"Excellent workshop! Bill was direct and on point. Though I came from a different Meetup group, I was so impressed I decided to join Bill's group. The room was overflowing and many stayed to ask Bill questions. . . ." *Oakland, CA*

"You have a great sense of humor and an easy public speaking technique!" *Campbell, CA*

"Your presentation full of great nuggets and very applicable advice needed to be shared outside the Sassy room—it was AWESOME!" *Campbell, CA*

" I stayed awake for the entire class! " *Sunnyvale, CA*

" I especially like your handouts. At first I thought it was silly that you had a fill in the blank format but that is what kept me engaged for the whole class." *Mountain View, CA*

"Overall, very informative + entertaining presentation. Thank you!" *San Jose, CA*

"Let's just say that after attending two lectures from Bill Belew, this one for the second time (I lost my notes from the first one), I am now a diehard Bill Belew groupie!!! When Bill Belew speaks, I take good notes, and I suggest you do too!" *Saratoga, CA*

"Lots of information. I came with my sister who knows a lot more about the subject than I do. We both came away with useful information. The speaker was passionate, well-informed, and gave away as much information as he could in the time allotted." *Berkeley, CA*

"I can't think of anything else, my mind is overwhelmed at the moment. I'm glad I got up early to be here." *Santa Clara, CA*

"I thoroughly enjoyed last evening's meeting in Palo Alto. Lots of useful content!!! So glad I purchased your book, too. I only wish I hadn't had to drive 2 hours home after a VERY long and involved day. Also wish you lived closer to Carmel area as I would attend as many of your Meet Ups as possible. BRAVO!" *Palo Alto, CA*

"Very informative—it proved so valuable that most of the audience lined up immediately after the talk to buy the presenter's book." *San Miguel, Mexico*

"All the content was great! Very well organized and helpful. Really got my creative juices flowing." *Campbell, CA*

"I really believe in Bill's technique. First of all, they make sense. Second of all, he shows us the proof—the record of hits and page views from his web hosting service. Third, what he proposes is not easy to do. It is simple, but not easy, and that is almost always the case with good advice!" *Mountain View, CA*

"Great speaker—funny and informative. Useful and valuable information." *Indianapolis, IN*

"All was helpful! I was so tired this morning that I almost didn't attend. I'm sooo glad I did." *San Francisco, CA*

"I have finally found a perfect platform to share my thoughts with others. Thank you very much. Now, how do I go about paying for your service?" *Sacramento, CA*

If the principles I teach here don't work for you, dinner is on me. Seriously. Dinner is on me. You can contact me through my personal web site—www.billbelew.com.

CHAPTER 3

5 Reasons Why Business Blogs Are King of Social Media

I like the cowboy philosopher Will Rogers. He and I are similar. We have the same first name.

We are different, too. The only account he likely ever balanced was his checking. I have Facebook, Twitter, LinkedIn, and Google+ accounts. I also own a blog network with 12 active sites, each with a login. And I provide content for a national media outlet. (The interested reader can check www.billbelew.com for a link to these sites—it's where I go each morning to remember where I am supposed to write.)

Will Rogers said, "If you can do it, it ain't bragging." To make my points in this chapter, I am going to have to do what might be construed by some as "bragging." It's not. Call it a case study. In this chapter I will share more real screen shots from real sites. I will even give a real peek into the earning potential of business blogs. Read that last sentence again. The blog does the work. The blog makes money.

Blogs are King of Social Media. Specifically business blogs. Facebook, Twitter, LinkedIn, and the other one, Google+, are just princes at best.

By the time you are done reading this chapter you will be convinced that you or your company or both need an active, dynamic blog as part of your social media strategy. Or if you already have a blog that it needs and can get more real and relevant traffic to your site. Real and relevant traffic being honest to goodness business leads.

Here are my four reasons why business blogs are King.

Reason #1 Why the Business Blog Is King—Bloggers Get Read by Readers They Know

If you have 500 or more connections on LinkedIn you are in the top 10–25 percent in terms of connections. I am in that top 10 percent http://www.linkedin.com/in/billbelew. And truth be told, I do NOT know all those people.

However, I have more than 6,000 subscribers to my blog. I **know** them. They are 18–34-year-old men, in college or grad school, who are single and primarily log on from home. They are also interested in. . . .

12 Facts about Web Traffic Professor Wil.by
Testimonials

1. Here's a Ripplemaker video a couple of Google Youtube folk made about Wil.by. The YT will give you just a little insight into who I am. The numbers are off as the video was created in early '11. My network of sites is well over 50.57 million page

I also have over 22,000 active email addresses in the same demographic that were given to me via my blog subscribe feature. When a blog owner allows readers to subscribe to receive email updates using a free service such as feedburner, readers give, that is, readers ask for email updates to arrive in their email boxes at intervals that the reader decides is best for him or her. And all the blogger has to do is write and hit publish. There are no email client charges associated such as might be found at an Aweber, Constant Contact, iContact, or MailChimp. Just write and hit publish.

Additionally I have exceeded 4,000 business types all located in the San Jose (yes, I know the way) area who follow me at Meetups where I teach/preach business blogging. I know these people. They are entrepreneurs, digital marketers, bloggers, writers, start uppers, web marketers, and . . .

On Facebook, Twitter, LinkedIn, and Google+ my followers, fans, contacts, and connections are . . . um, well, I am not sure.

My network of blogs garners enough visitors daily that I get solicitations, sometimes multiple times weekly, from advertisers asking me to put their ads on one or more of my sites to the readers I know.

Nobody has contacted me at Facebook, Twitter, LinkedIn, or Google+ asking me to put up ads . . . yet. And I am not holding my breath until they do.

> **POINT**—Bloggers with enough traffic can know the demographics of their readers. And this makes for good business opportunities. Knowing these demographics is not only good for potential advertisers but for the blog owner as well if he or she wants to sell something.

Reason #2 Why the Business Blog Is King—Bloggers Can Communicate with Their Readers

In my blog posts, I am not limited to 140 characters in my communication. And I cn pruv 2 ppl I no how 2 spel.

Additionally, my posts do not get buried in the feeds. And my archives are searchable.

Search this site

Search this website ...

SEARCH

Subscribe to receive emails

The average person spends four to five minutes on LinkedIn. More on Facebook. Less on Twitter. Most of that time is spent scrolling through messages or updates.

Funny thing, Facebook, Twitter, LinkedIn, and Google+ users want friends who have friends, right? But the more friends I have the quicker their updates go flying past my news feed at my sites, meaning the less I see! And the more friends my friends have the quicker my updates get buried on their feed! By any high estimate I have read, barely 3–5 percent of your fans see the content you post. What that means is that if you have 120 friends only 3.6 (that has to hurt that fourth person) people will see your updates. It is estimated that hairy men in leather at Harley-Davidson and pretty girls in skimpy underwear at Victoria's Secret see less than half of 1 percent of posts that happen at their Facebook fan page. Imagine—the active Facebook Social Media-ite must post 200 times at his or her Facebook fan page in hopes that maybe one person will read that post, much less act on it. And the optimal length of a Facebook post? Just 60 characters! That's about seven to eight words! At my blog sites, my readers get emails when I update it. I know who is reading what, which post(s) I wrote are being commented on, and I can respond accordingly by giving readers more or building on something that is being read. Invariably, good Facebook, Twitter, LinkedIn, and Google+ users will provide, in the form of a short link, a link to their site or the URL they are commenting about so the reader can get more information. That link goes . . . to their blog.

Chiefs don't accept gift-wrapped chance for win from Chargers, lose 20-17
http://t.co/A2AJxKno via Twitter

Chiefs don't accept gift-wrapped chance for win from Chargers, lose...
examiner.com
Admit it. Right before Chiefs quarterback Matt Cassel threw the game-ending interception to San Diego Chargers safety, Eric Weddle, on a screen pass...

Like · Comment · Send a message · Share · 28 minutes ago

is now connected to Niraj Brahmbhatt **and** Angelo Hatzistratis
Send a message · 31 minutes ago

5 Vanity Metrics to Stop Measuring (And Better Alternatives)
http://t.co/pvKYzth2 via @HubSpot via Twitter

5 Vanity Metrics to Stop Measuring (And Better Alternatives)
blog.hubspot.com
For marketing metrics, don't get caught up in vanity metrics - Here are 5 analytics you should stop obsessing over and better alternatives.

Like · Comment · Send a message · Share · 31 minutes ago

The princes of social media, Facebook, Twitter, LinkedIn, and Google+, do their best work when they are complemented by a good blog/web site. (Incidentally, I use the terms interchangeably. A blog is a web site is a blog.) At my blog posts, I can also provide links to other articles using real words that people can read and decide to click through and read . . . or not.

Tomorrow – Blogging for money – tip #1 – What kind of blogger are you?

Related Posts:

- Introduction to Blogging for Web Traffic – Key #1 of 4 to be successful
- Blogging for money and Web Traffic – tip #51 – Good content strategy #9 – the long tail
- Blogging for money and Web Traffic – tip #26 – why businesses & blogs fail
- Introduction to blogging for Web Traffic or 5 Reasons why I blog
- Blogging for money and Web Traffic – tip #41 – SEO technique #11 – building authority

converter and why a blogger needs to know

- Japan Tourism Agency offers 10,000 free tickets to Japan for influential bloggers
- Where to check your Google Page Rank. And does it really matter?
- Blogging is the platform of choice for writers in the High Desert
- What a Christian blogger, atheism and communism have in common

POINT—Bloggers can communicate with their readers.

Reason #3 Why the Business Blog Is King—Bloggers Can Be Found . . . Again and Again and Again

Indeed, the other social media can be searched. But not by the major search engines . . . yet.

More than two out of three people who come to my blogs come looking for me. Read that last sentence again. At 100,000 visits a day, that's like every student and faculty member at Ohio State University twice, coming to see what I am doing, every day, because they wanted something I offered. Who comes looking for you on your Facebook, Twitter, LinkedIn, and Google+ accounts? And how do you know?

A more accurate number is upwards of 80% of my visitors are people who are looking for me. The other 20% are people who already know me (direct traffic) or were sent to me (referral traffic). One other way to get people to your site is to pay them to come via adwords or some other such scam. I have NEVER ever paid for traffic. I remember learning that people could be bought/enticed to come via ads. It made me mad. Still does. And it makes some online advertisers very very rich, too. Can't fault the advertisers for that. But buying ads in hopes of getting people to come to your site is NOT the best way to get them there. Consider this, when you stop buying the ads, the visitors will stop coming. If you build good quality content into your sites, people will come for a long time even when you stop writing. More on that later.

PanAsianBiz	
Site Summary	
VISITS	
Total	14,042,680
Average Per Day	15,285
Average Visit Length	1:12
Last Hour	360
Today	132
This Week	106,994
PAGE VIEWS	
Total	21,269,811
Average Per Day	21,654

Greenpacks.org
Site Summary

VISITS

Total	2,785,790
Average Per Day	3,428
Average Visit Length	0:44
Last Hour	133
Today	2,613
This Week	23,998

PAGE VIEWS

Total	3,620,102
Average Per Day	4,711

FilmyFair
Site Summary

VISITS

Total	2,873,478
Average Per Day	2,250
Average Visit Length	1:49
Last Hour	123
Today	165
This Week	15,750

PAGE VIEWS

Total	4,143,754
Average Per Day	4,506

Do you know that web site owners that update their sites multiple times daily (read: web site owners who have an active blog in place) get 2.6 times as many leads as those with a static site? I think bloggers spend 2.6 less time goofing off on their blogs than users of Facebook, too!

Do you also know that inbound marketing is CHEAPER than outbound marketing? Creating a well-trafficked blog is much cheaper than going to a trade show. Attracting someone to your

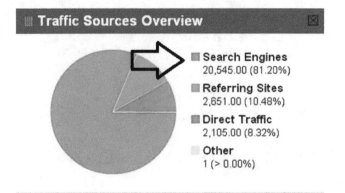

business blog is cheaper than direct mail. And applying good search engine optimization (SEO) strategies is cheaper than telemarketing.

I have a friend who lives on the right coast. At least twice a year he flies to San Francisco to participate in a trade show of some sort. He gets a booth that is perhaps 6 feet by 10 feet. He puts up a banner and passes out Halloween-sized bags of M&Ms and sponge brains in hopes of getting a business card that he can follow up on. The booth costs him $7,000 EACH time he comes + travel costs + hotel/food costs = $20,000? If savvy marketers will spend that much money to create a good blog and follow good practices they can get 20,000–200,000 good, real, and relevant traffic (read: people looking for them because they have what they want) and be miles ahead of other social media users and conference goers.

POINT—Bloggers get searched for AND found.

Reason #4 Why the Business Blog Is King—The Blog Makes Money

I work in social media and blogging is my preferred method. My blog makes money. If I feed content to this inanimate object, the blog will work for me, 24/7/365. And I don't have to provide it with health insurance. Revenue generated from traffic to my blog network ALONE pays my bills. In the time it takes the average reader to finish reading this chapter my blog will make enough money for me and my wife and daughter out to eat. In the time it takes to read the whole book - to Disneyland!

Income from ad revenue ALONE at my blogs is sufficient to pay my sizable Silicon Valley mortgage.

The accompanying image was captured after about six months from just one of my blog sites.

How much money did you make at your Facebook, LinkedIn, Google+, and Twitter accounts last year or last month or today? How much business did those princes of social media bring you?

And did I say that my blog is a platform for other services I provide—consulting, speaking, done for you service, membership site and so on?

Not only does the blog work for me, the blog is a tremendous source of lead generations for services or products that I want to offer. And the blog is a gift that keeps on giving those leads.

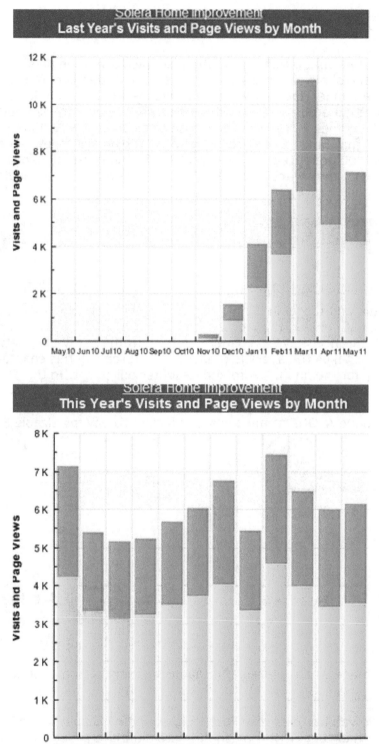

In the accompanying two images you can see that this home remodeler/client was able to grow traffic to his site month after month for about four months. This client told me that at the beginning he was getting maybe one bid a month on new projects. After four months he and his partner were averaging one bid a day! They got so busy he didn't have time to write. And for the next entire year he didn't write. But the traffic to his site dropped off only marginally and the leads and business opportunities kept on coming!

Here's an email blurb from the owner of this site. He was about to throw in the towel on his business and just blog. Instead . . .

> "Your SEO recipe is working and i'm [sic] running around doing bids for bathroom remodeling. We now average one bid request for a sizeable job a day, whereas before it was one a month and we were living on handyman work. We closed two bathroom remodel jobs this week alone, and are now in the process of bidding on a total of about 20. It's been keeping me busy."

Imagine that . . . your blog paying the bills, or some of them . . . AND bringing you work.

POINT—Make no mistake. Blogs make money. And business blogs done right bring business.

Reason #5 Why the Business Blog Is King—Blogs give a good return on investment of time

I understand that most would not consider sites like Digg, Newsvine, StumbleUpon, Redditt, Mixx, IndianPad and their ilk as social media sites. In my mind they are quite similar. They involve posting, voting (liking), commenting and hopes of more traffic to the home site (referrals). The more active the user the better the relationship with other users (sounds social to me) and the more referrals (traffic) to the home site in the long run.

I worked this well before Facebook, LinkedIn, Google+ and Twitter came around. Make no mistake, a website owner can 'drive' more traffic to their website if they work it hard. I was getting a couple of thousand views a month at the time and I multiplied this 10-fold to well over 20,000 views just by working the sharing sites. Working = posting, interacting, voting and commenting.

Yay, me! Right? Wrong.

I kept a log of how much time it took me to work the sharing sites and I knew how much more traffic I was getting as a result of my efforts AND how much money that traffic was earning me. Time spent getting me more traffic did result in growth. But I was earning a whopping $2.14/hour for my effort. For every hour I spent on the social sites I made an additional $2.14.

Additionally, besides the increase in traffic, the referral traffic from these sites was the worst. I measured this by the number of pages they turned. Referral traffic tends to come see what they have been sent to see and nothing else. Invariably they hit the backspace on their keyboard and are measured as a bounce. They came saw and left = didn't like what they saw enough to check out more. This might be the worst kind of traffic a web site can get. The only other traffic I can think that might be worse is traffic that has been paid for AND bounced.

Traffic from search engines bring people who have found your site because it has something or almost something they were looking for. The search engine user might look around, flip the pages and often click on relevant ads if your site doesn't address their query.

I reckon that I have spent at least 100 hours on Facebook and Google+. Probably more. I have yet to make $1000 from all of this effort. Maybe I am no good, but I don't think that's the problem. But suppose I did make $1000 for my 100 hrs of invested time. That's a whopping $10/hr. Not worth it. And what are the chances of making $10K or more from an impersonal connection made via social media. The bigger the amount, the more real face-to-face time that will be required adding to the number of hours spent.

Social media is good for branding at best. And not very good at that.

And when I stop working the social media channels, the traffic stops. That is, there is very little residual traffic from social media efforts. And the traffic that does come doesn't pay all that well. Long term residual traffic to a well-written blog post is good stuff and pays well.

POINT—Time spent on social media does not offer a good return on investment of time.

Conclusion:

Blogs are the King of social media.

The key, of course, is for them to be done well and attract relevant traffic. That is what this book is about—strategies for building a better business blog and getting more **FREE** organic traffic.

4 Keys to Get Serious Traffic to Your Web Site

As of this writing (December 2012), **more than 70 million unique visitors** have searched out and found one or more of the pages at my blogs/web sites. Those visitors have also flipped through more than **100 million pages**, enough for every person in the United Kingdom, France, Italy, or South Korea. Canada (three times), Australia (four times), Greece (nine times). There are only 11 countries in the world that have more people than I have had pages viewed at my sites. And ALL of them came because they were **looking for me**, for something I had that they wanted. I have NEVER paid for traffic . . . EVER. It is **ALL FREE**, organic, quality search engine traffic.

Question: How often does that happen on Facebook, Google+, LinkedIn, or Twitter?

www.facebook.com/TheTrafficProfessor

Not long ago, I recruited a very well-known Facebook guru to do a webinar to a sizable (4,000 +) group of business folk that have subscribed to learn from me. While we were waiting for the participants to come online, we had this short conversation.

> FB Guru, "Bill, what do you do exactly?"
> "I am a professional blogger."
> "Oh?"
> "During the course of your one-hour webinar my network of sites will make enough money to take me, my wife, and my daughter to the movies."
> "Wow!"
> I turned down the volume on my headset a bit and added, "And out to eat."
> "Holy cow! I need to learn how you do that!"

I should have turned down the volume more.

A good (read: well-trafficked) blog/web site not only serves as a platform to sell your services and to bring leads, but the blog itself can be a source of income.

Not long ago, in the space of one month I was at three conferences at San Jose, San Diego, and San Francisco. There were hundreds of booths and thousands of attendees who had paid well over 10 Benjamins to attend. They ALL had one thing in common: They ALL wanted more traffic to their sites so they could peddle their ideas, services, or wares. Business Facebook, Google+, LinkedIn, and Twitter users are the same; they, too, want people to come to their sites. Everyone wants more traffic. And that is what I will teach you here—**how to get more traffic.** Legitimate and relevant traffic.

The booths at these conventions lured foot traffic with promises of free iPad2s, wind-up robots, Frisbees, massages by girls in pink rabbit ears, and other goodies in exchange for email addresses or business cards. Facebook, Google+, LinkedIn, and Twitter experts also make promises and give gifts (discount codes, free webinars, white papers . . .) in hopes of getting that all-important email address so they can try AGAIN to get someone to come to their website. **People come looking for bloggers.**

Attendees at each of the three conferences also had high HOPES of partnering with someone who also MIGHT get them more exposure so that they POSSIBLY could better market their products (read: MAYBE get people to come to their web sites), by sharing their email lists with a prayer for people to come to, you guessed it, their web sites. That's okay but there's another way. A blog done well will absolutely have **people come searching** from the get-go.

Research says it is 62 percent cheaper to have someone come looking for you than it is for you to go looking for them. **Creating a well-trafficked blog** is much more cost efficient than shelling out money to set up a booth at a trade show and pay you and/or your employees to fly, drive, or walk there while putting those employees in a hotel and feeding them. **Applying good search engine optimization principles** to your dynamic web site (read: active blog) is much more effective and less costly than telemarketing. Less annoying, too! Exercising **good social media strategies** of which a blog is King (see the previous chapter) makes much more sense while costing less than direct mail.

The most pertinent questions are not:

> **"Should I** blog?"
> **"Should I** have a blog at my site?"
> **"Should I** create a dynamic site to draw attention to my product?"
> **"Should I** link my Facebook account to my blog?"

but

> **"How can I** learn to blog better?"

And

> **"What does it take** to get good, quality, relevant traffic to my web site?"

The answer to that last question in a broad sense follows. I will go into the actual mechanics in subsequent chapters.

Here are **four absolutes every blog must have in order to get traffic to the site.**

▪ 1. A Website must have a Sufficient QUANTITY of Articles/Posts to Get Noticed

Clients have told me they have 30 articles or pages at their site and wondered aloud, "Why isn't anyone finding me?" Other clients say the same about their 300 posts.

I have more than 30,000 posts.

Call it the "duh" factor. But it is absolutely fundamental—the more stuff you have at your web site, the more findable you are. I have a thousand times greater possibility of being found than some people. Of course, if your goal is to reach a local market, you don't need 30,000 articles. You just need more pages/articles/posts than anyone else in your local niche who is competing for the same search engine ranking that you are. Simple as that.

I was talking to a guy the other day who wants to create a site about being an expert witness. My advice to him was to do a search for "expert witness" in his area. Check the top results in the search engines and go to that site. Count the number of pages at that site and do more. He will outrank his competitor. Provided, of course, that he takes into consideration the other three absolutes here.

Site	# of posts	Traffic	Traffic/post
A	533	836,464	1,569.3
B	372	494,066	1,328.1
C	240	167,024	695.9

The accompanying chart shows real results of three sites with the same search engine findability. Site A had 2.2 times the number of posts in the same time period as site C, but saw more than 5 times the traffic. There is a point where doing more than your competitor will give you a LOT better results.

Too often bloggers will think that if they write half of what their competitor does, they can make half the income or get half the traffic. That mindset simply is not always true.

Rather, I tell my students to find the volume of posts that they must write for their niche till they can see the exponential results they desire. Sometimes, doing twice what the next guy is doing will get you five times the results.

> **Lesson**: Do more posts/updates than your competitor and you will get better results. Simple, eh?

But it's not just "stuff." You need quality.

2. A Website must have GOOD-QUALITY Articles

Good quality means the articles are written in such a way as to **appeal to the search engines AND to the readers.** I have heard from one of the top search engine engineers that there are some 220 variables that go into how a page or a site is ranked. However, I have also learned there are only about 20 parameters that, if employed correctly, will give a web site owner up to 90–95 percent of a site's search engine results. The other 200 items will help improve a site's effectiveness by 5–10 percent. Problem is, people want to spend their time fiddling with the other 200 rather than working the 20 to get the most for their effort.

I preach at a church in Silicon Valley. One of my members worked for the world's most popular search engine for about three years in that company's blogging platform development. When I told him about the 20 parameters getting 90 percent of the results I want, he said it was more like 10 parameters.

Interestingly enough, this fellow went on to start his own company; that happens a lot here in the Valley. He took me out to lunch to pick my brain on the 20.

> This?
> "Look at me. My 10 articles and my web pages that have perfect SEO. I just wish someone would read them."
> Or this?
> "Hundreds of people are asking me in the comments for more information about [insert your service here]."
> What are the 20? Keep reading.

Here's one tip: Write an article of a couple hundred words and save it in a random folder on your desktop. Then wait for a couple of weeks. Then go and find it.

Can't find it? What do you do? Use the desktop search function.

Imagine what words you would put into a search engine box to find the information you wrote about. Use those words in your title.

Cute, spiffy, and clever doesn't work. Seldom do people put an adjective or adverb in a search engine box. No conjunctions, no articles, no prepositions. Clunky but reader friendly works best. Use good titles and you will be leaps and bounds ahead of the guy who is deciding where and when to use an H2 header, or which words should be boldface or italicized and which should not.

PanAsianBiz	
Entry Pages Ranked by Visits	
	Entry Page
478	http://www.panasianbiz.com/asi...xposes-undergraduate-students/
403	http://www.panasianbiz.com/edu...yderabad-jntu-ac-results-html/
324	http://www.panasianbiz.com/asia/india/jntu-hyderabad-results/
169	http://www.panasianbiz.com/wor...ked-sara-jean-performing-yoga/
117	http://www.panasianbiz.com/ent...ran-johars-party-photos-video/
92	http://www.panasianbiz.com/mob...-review-features-photos-video/
86	http://www.panasianbiz.com/tec...eview-specifications-features/
73	http://www.panasianbiz.com/ad/jntu-ac-results-html/
72	http://www.panasianbiz.com/asi...dianrail-irtc-railway-enquiry/
70	http://www.panasianbiz.com/edu...baroda-results-2011-announced/
69	http://www.panasianbiz.com/ent...es-specifications-photo-video/
65	http://www.panasianbiz.com/ind...p-of-china-the-15-most-useful/
43	http://www.panasianbiz.com/asi...st-know-facts-about-india-map/
41	http://www.panasianbiz.com/cat...cation/exam-results-education/
40	http://www.panasianbiz.com/asi...ds-2011-winners-photo-gallery/
34	http://www.panasianbiz.com/
34	http://www.panasianbiz.com/asi...key-gate-forum-solved-general/

The posts circled in the accompanying screen capture were written years ago and they still get hundreds of views daily. Good-quality posts will rank highly in the search engines for a very long time!

I had a client who is a really good writer. He does a much better job of getting his point across than I while also entertaining the reader in the process. He writes about hiking at www.hike-halfdome.com.

I gave him one quick pointer.

> "Put the name of the mountain or trail that you are writing about in your title."
> He did.
> Just two weeks later there was a terrible accident on one of the mountains he was particularly familiar with. The phone rang.
> National news station: "Are you the writer of this article?"
> Client: "Yup, that's me."
> "We'd like to interview you on national television. You seem to be the expert on this mountain."

Fast forward . . . he is now getting a lot of calls and speaking engagements including one from a Japanese station that wants him to guide them up a mountain. All because he knew how to add quality to his blogs. That is, he began to consider how to add appeal to real people AND the search engines to his posts.

Lesson: Good-quality writing appeals to real people and to the search engines. It is not as subjective as you think.

▨ 3. A Blog Site must be CONSISTENTLY Updated

Depending on your traffic goals and the size of the market you are appealing to, daily works. Multiple times a day works better. I know sites that update hourly and even several times an hour. They have a worldwide audience and their traffic reflects their effort and consistency. The answer for you is to **update your site more often than your competitor does**.

Bill Belew	Recent Visitors by Visit Details			
Detail	Domain Name	Visit Time	Page Views	Visit Length
1	comcast.net	Jan 10 2011 6:29:53 am	1	0:00
2	sbcglobal.net	5:10:25 am	1	0:00
3	comcast.net	2:37:19 am	1	0:00
4	74.125.16.#	1:23:23 am	1	0:00
5	webspeed.dk	Jan 9 2011 11:15:13 pm	1	0:00
6	comcast.net	10:38:44 pm	2	0:00
7	comcast.net	9:17:52 pm	3	6:16
8	googlebot.com ⇐	3:11:15 pm	1	0:00
9	comcast.net	2:13:02 pm	18	24:08
10	comcast.net	2:08:28 pm	2	0:06
11	122.248.183.#	2:04:42 pm	1	0:00
12	comcast.net	10:05:13 am	1	0:00
13	comcast.net	9:09:06 am	1	0:00
14	comcast.net	8:52:11 am	1	0:00
15	comcast.net	8:48:10 am	6	1:37
16	googlebot.com ⇐	5:47:37 am	1	0:00
17	comcast.net	4:51:57 am	2	1:45

And you want to update your site until you start getting the results you want.

Fundamentally, the more often a website is updated, the more often the searchbots come to see what is going on. The more often the bots come, the more they think (if bots could think) something new is here, resulting in a step up in search engine ranking appeal. Makes sense?

If you don't update your site in the form of a new post or even comments to exisiting posts, why would a searchbot come back much less a real person?

Search engines cannot make subjective determinations on whether a site is good or bad. A search engine will, however, interpret an update as more relevant.

Add a sitemeter, it's free. Check your sitemeter and see when the last time the googlebot came to visit you. Can't find the googlebot? Ask yourself how often you update your site.

Lesson: Find out how often your competitor updates his or her site and update yours more often. Provided you have a depth of archives and good-quality posts, your site will outrank them.

There's one more criteria.

■ 4. A Website must Stay with it LONG ENOUGH to Catch On

A blog must have longevity. Quantity can be controlled; just do more. Quality can be controlled; just do better. Consistency can be controlled; just do it more often. Longevity has to be earned.

I have learned that the **number one reason why businesses fail** is that the business doesn't or can't stay around till the idea catches on. Not enough seed money. Supplier goes missing. Divorce. Relocation. Earthquake! Whatever. Something comes up to keep the business from continuing. If the business was a good idea at the beginning, it's more often than not a good idea to dog it until it catches on . . . no matter what.

Walt Disney: "Get a good **idea** and stay with it. **Dog it**, and work at it until it's done right."

Disney made the world fall in love with a mouse! I had a student from China that I taught when I lived in Japan. It was not long after China began to open up that I took her to a ice cream shop that was giving away little Snoopy and Charlie Brown key chains?

"Who's this?"
"Um, that's Snoopy and Charlie Brown."
"Who are they?"

She didn't know Snoopy! But she knew who Mickey Mouse was.

A blog is no different. Think in terms of months to get the best results. To be sure, ranking, exposure, and traffic can be achieved in a short time. But they can and usually do disappear just as quickly.

The longer it takes to build something up, the longer it takes for it to disappear.

(There is a point when a site will catch on and the traffic takes off.)

Not a few people will work hard at their sites for three, four, five, even six months. They will post 100–150 articles a month and after three months or 450 posts, five or six months of 600–750 posts, conclude,

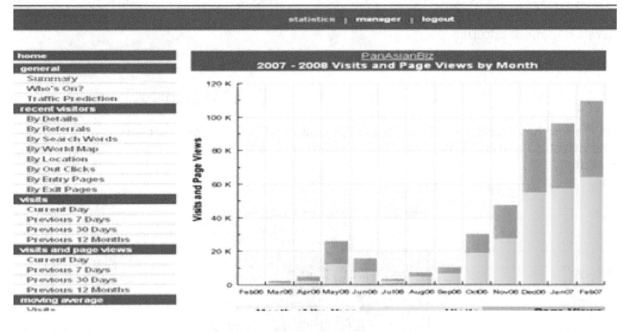

"Bill lied to me."

Then they quit.

This happened to me not long ago. The client invested several thousand dollars over four months. Traffic was coming but in spits and spurts. But it was good search engine traffic. He gave up when he should have been thinking 'how can I better convert the traffic that is coming?' and 'how can I find a way to stay faithful to this process?'

Sometimes it might take 10 months.

Nothing is more important than resolving to stick with your blog till it catches on.

Lesson: If you're giving up, first ask yourself how long have you have been at it and how hard have you tried? Stay with it.

Super Bowl namesake Vince Lombardi put it this way. "The harder you try, the harder it is to give up."

Chances are that if you are ready to give up on your blog, it is because you haven't put enough effort into it. Think of it as the longer you are left waiting on hold on a telephone call, the harder it is to hang up. Of course, there are times when you might want to cut your losses. But as for me, I don't know when that is.

In the meantime. Get started. Get started today. Do it now. Before dinner. Get an online presence, write something, and start building your longevity.

The Big Questions

Of course, everyone wants to know:

1. Regarding QUANTITY—how many posts do I need to write?
2. Regarding QUALITY—what are those 20 must-knows?
3. Regarding CONSISTENCY—how often is often?
4. Regarding LONGEVITY—how long does it take to catch on?

These are questions that I will answer in the remainder of this book. I will tell you **how many posts**, **how many words**, **how many days** overall and at **what pace** I wrote to see the first 1,000,000 visitors to my sites. Use my metrics as a signpost or measuring stick or benchmark and apply yourself accordingly. A person who gets 1,000,000 visitors can most always tell you how to get 100,000 or 10,000 visitors to come. The reverse of that is not true. Scaling down is a whole lot easier than scaling up. Whereas, just doubling the effort does not always give twice the results.

If your ideas are good, why shouldn't people know about them?

If your insights are really good, you might even have a moral obligation to get the word out.

There are 34,000 searches done every second!

More than 2,000,000 searches are done each minute and as many as 3 billion searches are done EACH day.

Why shouldn't people be finding you?

It's not hard. It's not easy.

The hard part is being faithful till your idea catches on. And it will catch on.

Blogging is **a way to be found,** to have **people come looking for you**.

5 Biggest Obstacles to Getting Your Blog Started and What to Do to Overcome Them

In my years of blog consulting with veteran, newbie, and wannabe bloggers I have learned that there are generally five big obstacles that most bloggers face in getting their blog started.

In this chapter I will not only share those five obstacles, I will also give the reader the solutions to overcome them.

I am not "horn tooting" here. But I have received more than 10,000 readers in a lifetime, in a year, in a month, in a day, in an hour, and in a minute. I know what kind of web site it takes and what kind of effort is required. By the way, it is not super-human effort either. I also know what does NOT need to be done and where time does NOT necessarily need to be spent.

I say again I want the reader to have confidence that what I have learned and share here comes not from theory but from real-world experience helping more people create web sites than I can remember.

The obstacles and the solutions.

Obstacle #1 to Getting Started with Your blog—Picking a Domain Name

I am genuinely surprised at the number of times that I have sat with small businesses or corporate clients who were paying me from $200 to $500 an hour (really!) to discuss with them what domain name they should use.

I suppose it is natural to think that some names might be better than others, and it is best to choose the most ideal name.

The simple truth—it really doesn't matter what your domain name is. I have some very stupid names for some of my sites and they still have received anywhere from 1 to 30 million page views total, depending on the topic.

Question: Why is that?

Answer: The domain name is not nearly as important as your tagline, your choice of categories, the title you choose on individual posts, and the consistent relevance of your content to the overall theme of your blog. Get these latter points right and you can call your blog anything you want.

That being said, I do have some suggestions.

1. Choose Something People can Spell

Americans are pretty much spelling challenged. If you were not born between 1954 and 1959, you probably are not that good at putting all your letters in a row correctly. From 1954 to 1959 Americans learned how to spell phonetically. I can spell things I have never heard or seen before (usually) and I can guess at the pronunciation of most words. Yeah, I am old. I know it. My brother was born in 1953. He can't spell to save his soul. My sister was born in 1960. Yup, can't spell.

Not long ago the world's largest domain and hosting provider invited me to their HQ for a tour and some priming. I'll explain below. One of the things I learned was that the average length of a domain name is eight or nine characters. This company would know, right?. They have sold some 53 million domain names and the hosting to go with it.

Choose something that is as short as possible and that people can spell.

2. Use Your Own Name

I own BillBelew.com. It is not because I am vain. It is because it's me. As I mentioned earlier, it was also the name of Elvis Presley's costume designer. If you happen to have the name of somebody famous, good for you. Most don't. And even you do, it's not all that helpful in the long run. I met a woman who owns www.vanilla.com. She still can't get traffic or figure out how to monetize it.

Incidentally, do you know the two most common ways to become a famous blogger?

1. Become famous, then start writing a blog.
2. Write a blog, then become famous.

For the most part, if you can't think of a good domain name that hasn't been used in 10 minutes or less, use your own name. Add your middle initial if you must. Add your title. First initial, last name. First name, last initial. That sort of thing. I can't emphasize enough the importance of choosing something for your domain name to just get started. See the previous chapter and the section on longevity.

3. You can always change your domain name.

My son is a concert pianist and fine artist who started getting pretty popular. People starting asking him if he had a web site. When he told them the name (it was an old fantasy character), the response was "Huh?"

> Repeat the name.
> "Huh?"
> He finally bought the name BenjaminBelew.com and used a redirect to the old website domain name. Nobody knows the difference unless they check the URL box at the top AFTER they type in the domain name.
> Who does that?
> Curious?
> Type in www.benjaminbelew.com and see how it changes.
> Pick a name and get started. Do it now.

Obstacle #2 to Getting Started with Your blog—Choosing Good/Reliable/Cheap Hosting

At least half the world's population are shoppers. Everyone wants to know where is the best place to get the most reliable hosting at the cheapest price.

Answer: Short of someone subsidizing the costs, the cheapest place to go is www.bm2hosting .com

Full disclosure: I own this, but keep reading before you pass judgment on what may seem to be self-promotion here.

I bought the rights to be a reseller for the world's largest domain and hosting company. See above. I asked, "What is the lowest possible price I can sell domains and hosting for without me having to dip into my own pocket to pay?"

Those are the prices at BM2Hosting.

When people buy there, I do not make any money. Seriously, I pay a nominal sum annually (about the cost of a month's worth of gasoline for my car) to be able to resell these products so that my students and clients will not get bogged down searching for something better, cheaper, more dependable. There isn't anything better.

Key qualifications:

---

1. Nowhere more cheaply
2. 24/7 support—great customer service.
3. Solid reputation

Somebody, someplace might sell a domain name or hosting more cheaply in the beginning, but rest assured they will get you on the back end. Nobody is in the business of selling domain names and hosting to lose money.

Pick a domain name. Now buy it. Get hosting. Do it now.

This might be a good place to explain why you might want to fork out the $3-5/month for paid hosting. Nobody will take serious a blogger/website owner who is doing business on a free site. Think of it as setting up a lemonade stand in somebody else's front yard. For $75+ you can have your own domain and hosting and be in business online.

For those who don't know the difference between having a domain name and hosting, a domain name is like the address on the front of your house. The hosting is what goes on inside the house. Your content has to 'live' somewhere. Your computer is not hooked up to the internet 24/7/365, nor should it be. This is why you pay the coffee cup money monthly to have your content on a computer in some dark somewhat cool room outside of Phoenix. The rooms are cool, too! I have been there.

Obstacle #3 to Getting Started with Your Blog—Selecting the Best Software/Template

There is Blogger and **WordPress** and Typepad and Homemade.

The world's largest search engine's chief of search engine findability and spam prevention recommends WordPress. He uses a WordPress blog. And he says that WordPress templates are search engine friendly "out of the box." And this guy has all of that search engine's blogging resources at his disposal! He says to **use WordPress**. Do I need to continue?

Solution:Use WordPress because it has:

1. More flexibility—if you can think of something you'd like to have/do at your blog, somebody has figured out a way to do it.
2. More options—too many! People get lost exploring their options instead of hitting publish. There are countless plug-ins, widgets, and templates and any combination of the three.
3. Ease of use—If you can write an email, you can use WordPress.
4. Availability of help—There is a whole industry of worker bees helping people with their WordPress blogs. Don't know whom to ask? Ask me.

Question: Which WordPress template should you use?

Answer: If you can't decide within 15 minutes of looking at the many FREE options that WordPress offers, choose the default template and go with it for now.

The simple truth—in the beginning it doesn't matter what your site looks like, nobody is coming anyway. What is important is getting started. See the previous thoughts on longevity, the one item you cannot control.

Choose a template, start writing, and hit publish . . . often.

Obstacle #4 to Getting Started with Your Blog—Choosing What to Write About

Question: "What is the single best way to get more traffic to your web site?"

Answer: "Write more."

It is absolutely fundamental that the more you write, that is, the more often you hit the publish button, the higher the probability of AND the more actual visits you will see. Nothing beats publishing more. Period. Unless it would be writing more and better, using good SEO principles. See the previous chapter.

Solution: I tell people to write about something that:

1. They are interested in—Usually when people ask me what they should write about, they mean to ask what the highest paying niches are. I know the answer. But why would you want to write about something you don't care about just so you can make more money? Why not get a job you don't like just so you can be paid?
2. They can create an interest in—Write about your topic so much that people will think, "Hey, I'd better go see what all the fuss is about." A good hard-working blogger really can create his or her own "celebrity" status.
3. Is timeless—This is stuff that is always on people's "to-know" list: 5 of these, 4 reasons for, How to . . ., 6 Steps to . . ., and so on.
4. Is timely—What does what you know have to do with what is going on in the world around you? Make the connection.
5. They have a lot to say about—I tell my clients they need to write about something when have 1,000 things to say about it. Literally a thousand. Don't have that much to say? You will be hard pressed to make money blogging from traffic alone. Your blog can still work for you but you will need to have something to sell - a product or a service. And you will generally be limited to a local market.

Obstacle #5 to Getting Started with Your Blog—It's Too Much Work

Making a living blogging is a lot of work. Getting good results from (getting a LOT of traffic at your blog) is a lot of work. Doing better business, getting more leads, more clients, more offers from your blog is a lot of work. But if you don't want to work hard, I have solved that problem, too.

Solution: Write a big (depending on your goals) check and I will do it for you. And if not me, there are people who will ghost blog for you. But it costs money. And trust me, not everybody knows what they are doing.

Here is a blog post I wrote about this -

5 Qualities to look for in a blog consultant

What makes a good blog consultant? Who do you listen to when it comes to blogging? Here are 5 qualities I can think of.

1. A good blog consultant has put in his/her time.

Ask your blog consultant how many posts they have written. And how many of those posts have received how many views? What has s/he tried that did NOT work? I have published more than 12,000 posts. I have a couple of thousand articles/posts that have received more than 1000 views each. I have some others I am embarrassed about.

2. A good blog consultant knows how to get readers.

My very first month of blogging–March '06, I got 2,209 page views. The second month 4,595 views. Last month, my network of blogs got 1.3 million views, down a bit from December's total of 1.6 million.

3. A good blog consultant has been through the best of times and worst of times.

I started blogging for the KnowMoreMedia blog network in March of '06. I was with KMM till they peaked out at about 2 million views monthly at which time they fell out of love with the search engines and slowly died off. I wrote a lot for a lot, I have also written a lot for nothing. Ad revenues have been quite pitiful of late, but not as bad as they once were. Even so, I kept blogging away. My philosophy–when times are good I'd better work hard. When times are bad, I'd better work hard. Then when good times come back I'll be ahead of the crowd.

4. A good blog consultant can apply his/her principles across topics.

I have taken 10 different topics to above 1 million views each. A couple to more than 2 million and a couple more to over 4 million views . . . EACH. India, China, Japan, Education, Christian, Cricket, Environment and Bollywood. Some bloggers know what works for them, their blog and their niche, but do they know what works across the various topics. I do.

5. A good blog consultant will be there when you need them.

Here is my contact info. I'll be starting my fifth year as a blogger, paying my sizable Silicon Valley mortgage with my blogging revenue. If you are in the area, you are welcome to come by. I'll be there.

There is no reason why you can't get started blogging today. You can go from zero to hitting the publish button in about two hours.

The five biggest obstacles to getting started blogging are overcome:

1. Name—done.
2. Hosting—done.
3. Template—done.
4. Content—done.
5. Hard—done.

What are you waiting for? Get started today. Do it now.

CHAPTER 6

10 Things to Consider When Starting a Blog

I am convinced.

I can write enough pages in this book to lose your interest. That's not what I want to do here. It is my sincere desire to tell you what you need to know to get a blog started and get it read. I do NOT want to tell you everything there is to know. (I might write another book on the whys. But this is the how to version) Also, I don't know everything. I don't know a LOT of things, for that matter. But I do know what worked for me and what can work for you. I also know some things that aren't worth knowing for blogging success.

For example, I mentioned earlier that I have learned from one of the search engine's chief of spam prevention that there are some 220 parameters that go into search engine algorithms. But I have also learned that only about 20 of those parameters, if done well, will get you about 90-95 percent of the results you desire. I will focus on the 20 and getting them right instead of getting bogged down in the other 200.

What I mean to say is, if I don't write about something in this book, it's not all that important at this point.

In this chapter— let's discuss 10 things to consider when starting out as a serious blogger.

Are there other ways to start a blog than what I'll tell you here?

Yup.

Are there other free blog platforms than I'll list here?

Yup.

Are there better hosts for your blogs than I know about?

Maybe. If so, please let me know.

I want to get you started. I don't want you bogged down in not being able to decide how to start or which software to use or what name to use or which template is best or where to host or even what to write about.

I am going to have to stop giving out my real email address at workshops. After one workshop, one lady wrote to me so many times I finally had to tell her, "That was your last question. You have reached your quota. No more, please. The right answer to most questions is to make a decision, then make that decision work. There is not always a best way to do things. But there is a worst way. The worst decision is making no decision—no start."

Here are 10 things to consider when starting out as a serious blogger.

1. Do I Go It Alone?

By this I mean, do you choose a freebie blog (Put "free blog" in a search engine box and you'll get choices. I'll give you my preference below) and start writing and hope for the best? Or is there another way? Going it alone is doable, but there are tremendous advantages to starting off as part of a network. Going it alone, you have to find others to link to and hope they find you, or follow up on the comment you left at their blog site, or answer the email you sent them, or respond to all the comments left at your blog and the emails people send you. Not impossible, but hard. The more a blog is linked to other blogs that are linked to other blogs, the more findable a blog is. This is extremely important and I will explain why later. The independent blogger must find people to link to and find other bloggers to link to him or her. This means less time for writing and more time for schmoozing is needed.

Do I become part of a network?

Yes. Repeat after me. Yes. Yes. The advantages far outweigh the disadvantages.

Here's a blog post from www.billbelew.com

5 reasons to write for a blog network instead of going it alone. I have been asked not a few times—"What are the reasons/benefits, or why would a blogger want to be a part of a blog network as opposed to going it alone?" Here are a few:

1. Blogging alongside folk who have "been there done that" can save a LOT of time and energy for the individual blogger who otherwise would have to learn things all over again, to reinvent the wheel so to speak.
2. Which sounds better—I get a couple hundred/thousand unique visitors a day/month or I am part of a blog network that gets 50,000–75,000 unique visitors/day or 1.5–2 million page views a month?
3. Being a part of a blog network gives the blogger instant visibility. No begging to be linked to . . . you will already have access to other bloggers.
4. Having a tech support team do all the "fiddling" behind scenes frees the blogger up to do what they are supposed to do best—provide content.
5. Need someone to interview, guest blog? How about someone in the same network as you? A better question I think is—why should a blog network want to include you? What do you have to bring to other committed folk who want to provide something unique, add to the discussion at large?

If you can, find a network that will have you. I'll tell you how in a moment.

The biggest potential disadvantage to belonging to a network is that the content you create may belong to the owners of the network. Make sure you find out.

How?

Ask whoever welcomed you or is trying to sign you up to the network, "Does the content belong to me?"

Generally, if you are paid per post as I was in the beginning, the content will belong to the network owners. If you have a traffic-based revenue share (you get paid by how many people show up and a portion of how much money the site makes), the content will most likely belong to you.

I wrote for a network in the beginning and was paid per post. I eventually had to buy my content back from that network in order to make the sites, domains, and content my own.

2. What's My Name?

The name of your blog doesn't really matter that much. Of course, if you can get www .toyota.com or www.house.com and so on, by all means get them. Good luck with that. Many, most, if not all the good names are gone. Rather, build your own name. I discussed this in the previous chapter on overcoming obstacles to getting started.

Pick a name, any name. The most important thing to consider: pick something that people can spell and something that is memorable. That's it. When all else fails, use your own name. You can always change it later.

The domain name is not all that important. No name is a nonstarter. Pick something and make it work.

3. What's My Tagline?

Taglines are far more important than your domain name for your blog. What is the focus of your blog? In 10 words or less, what is your blog about? What words will people type in a search engine box that might bring them to you? This is important. My tagline at PanAsianBiz:

PanAsianBiz Dashboard Tagline: News in Asia—politics, movies, music, sports, business.

When a search engine comes crawling the little searchbots will be looking for the tagline. If the tagline of your blog is vague or ambiguous, the search engines won't know if they want to keep looking or not. Even if you say please. Search engines are dumb like that. Having a rock solid tagline also keeps you focused. A tagline is something you can tell a person between two floors on an elevator ride that will let them know what you write about.

Rule of thumb when determining a tagline: Think of something you can say 1,000 things about. Seriously. Not 160 or even 340, but 1,000. If you can't think of 1,000 things to say about your tagline, you are likely to run out of material over time. Of course, if you have a small market and a small group that you are trying to reach in a limited locale, that's a different story.

4. What Are My Categories?

The next most important thing to decide is your categories. The focus of your blog will be divided into categories, 10–15 at the most. The longer a blog lives, the more likely you are to have too many categories. Not good! I know this, too, from experience.

The URL of a blog post will include the domain name, the category the post is in, and the title of the post. Searchbots want these to be relevant to the tagline. Not only can searchbots be dumb, they can be persistent, too. The content of your post needs to be relevant to your title, category, and tagline. No fair coming up with a great title on five ways to make $1,000 in an hour, then write about the second coming of Jesus and how money won't be needed then anyway.

Rule of thumb when creating categories: A category is something you can think of 100 things to write about. Not 10 or 20.

5. What Software Will I Use?

There are a lot of options but only one choice. There is Blogger, Tumblr, Typepad, Moveable Type, something homemade, and WordPpress. Choose WordPress. WordPress is written for bloggers by bloggers. WordPress has a lot of Word Camps that go on from time to time, and meetup groups where WordPress nerds get together and solve problems. I have used both Blogger and WordPress and I don't use Blogger anymore. Sooner or later you are going to want your own site, have your own hosting, and it seems to me WordPress can make that transition go more smoothly. Most hosting companies have one-button WordPress installation. WordPpress is the software of choice. It is user friendly. It is flexible. It is powerful. It is free. Repeat after me - WordPress. For more on this see the previous chapter on overcoming obstacles.

6. Pick Your Look (Template)

Flowers, oceans, cute, techie, funky. WordPress gives you a LOT of choices. It's actually kind of fun to decide what your site will look like, IF you can make decisions. If choices overwhelm you, then ask a friend. Remember, the worst decision is no decision. Choose one. You can make changes later if you like. You will find options at the dashboard where you login to Word-Press. It's pretty intuitive, which means girls are better at it than guys . . . but not always. For what it's worth, I'd go with the default template in the beginning for the simple reasons I mentioned in the previous chapter. "Who cares what your template looks like. Nobody is coming anyway." Once people start showing up at your site, then you can fiddle with the look (template).

7. Where to Put the Sitemeter

Not having a sitemeter is like riding a bicycle without an odometer or driving a car without a gas gauge. Remember my '61 VW I wrote about previously? No gas gauge. Seriously. Since then, I have not been without a meter to tell me how far I've gone or need to go. A sitemeter is free and available at www.sitemeter.com. It will tell you where people came from, what they searched to get to your site, how long they stayed, and how many pages they read on average while they were there. You can also learn a lot about your readers: their countries, time zones, and other meaningless, um, useful facts. I could NOT have, still could NOT survive without my sitemeter. And if you belong to a network, chances are the tech folk will install it for you . . . for free. You can't beat that with a stick. Going it alone, you are on your own. And all the time you spend in the back end of your blog is not blogging. It's fiddling. You will feel as if you are getting stuff done, but if you aren't putting up content, you aren't blogging. You're fiddling. The sitemeter is pretty much the only fiddling I recommend. There are pretty easy instructions to follow at sitemeter.com. How to install a sitemeter is beyond the scope of this book. I'll try not to say that too often.

8. BM2Hosting.com vs. Blogger.com vs. WordPress.com

Sooner or later the serious blogger will want to have paid hosting. Think sooner. Paying for something is like investing in it. And the more you invest (time and/or money)in your blog, the more likely you will give the blog its due.

Consider this the next time you plan to quit anything. If you've put a LOT into it you aren't likely to abandon it too easily. Marriage, relationships, business. Even blogging.

Indeed, the more you put into your blog, the more likely you will see it through. It's the difference between riding a bike someone gives you and paying $1,500 for a bike.

BM2Hosting.com is my own hosting account. Use it. The reasons are in the previous chapter.

9. bill@billbelew.com

That is my real email address. Email me and I will consider you for my network. I will not own your content. We will do some sort of revenue share ONLY if you make money and ONLY if your site is worth including. If you make nothing, you owe me nothing. Can't beat that with a stick either. But you have to ask me. I am not going looking for you.

10. Blogging Jobs

Http://www.billbelew.com/subcribe is my site. Come to me. Contact me. Ask me. And I will help you get a job as a blogger. The jobs will be real and if you can pitch yourself and your blog idea, you can become part of a network.

Here is an exercise for you. After filling in the blanks, find five other bloggers or would-be bloggers to help you choose a name, a tagline, and 10 categories that will never go away.

Blog Exercise 1

What will I call my blog?

#1 _____

#2 _____

#3 _____

What's my tagline (focus)?

#1 _____

#2 _____

#3 _____

What are my categories?

#1 _____

#2 _____

#3 _____

#4 _____

#5 _____

#6 _____

#7 _____

#8 _____

#9 _____

#10 _____

Take these 10 considerations seriously before anyone will ever take you seriously as a blogger.

CHAPTER 7

22 Reasons Why You Might Want to Blog

It's funny (to me) that I am writing this chapter while watching the Super Bowl. Apparently the Super Bowl advertisers know (better than I) what I should be doing, drinking, wearing, reading, driving, putting under my arms, on my head, in my car, or on my face.

I do not for a moment think that everybody really SHOULD blog. But there are some folk who ought to give blogging serious consideration—writers (the kind that want to sell their books, build their platforms), speakers (the kind that want to motivate, sell, get their word or the WORD out), and others that I listed up in the preface of the book. If you have something you want a lot of people to know about, then blogging is one way to do that, and a good way, at that.

In 2009, one of the head honchos (pronounced *hoen choh* if you want to say it right, not *hahn choh,* as if that matters to most) of Technorati gave a presentation at Blog World Expo in Las Vegas. Technorati describes itself this way:

> ". . . the leading blog search engine, Technorati.com indexes millions of blog posts in real time and surfaces them in seconds. The site has become the definitive source for the top stories, opinions, photos and videos emerging across news, entertainment, technology, lifestyle, sports, politics and business. Technorati.com tracks not only the authority and influence of blogs, but also the most comprehensive and current index of who and what is most popular in the Blogosphere."

They are right. Technorati is all those things, and the serious blogger will visit Technorati often.

The Blog World Expo (BWE) was held annually in New York and Los Angeles. It has subsequently become New Media Live and become an annual event again as of 2013. The organizers say that BWE/NMX Live is "the first and only industry-wide tradeshow, conference, and media event dedicated to promoting the dynamic industry of new media including Blogging."

At BWE's website you can learn these blog statistics:

1. Over 12 million American adults currently maintain a blog. What that means is that almost one in every 10 Americans who go online do so to blog. Look around you. How many people can you count? Ten or more? One of them has a blog. Is it you?
2. More than 147 million Americans use the Internet. That's almost half. Next time you go to church, remember all the people on one side of the church are online at some time or other.
3. In 2008 half of the world's Internet population read blogs. In 2010 the number was two out of three!
4. Over 57 million Americans read blogs. At least two players in every basketball game, four in every football game, or the infield in every baseball game read blogs.
5. 1.7 million American adults list making money as one of the reasons they blog. I have made six figures (eight if you include beyond the decimal point!) blogging.
6. 89 percent of companies surveyed say they think blogs will be more important in the next five years. This only means something depending on the companies and how many were surveyed overall.
7. Companies with a blog have 4.2 times more pages indexed than companies without.

8. Pew Internet says 9 percent of internet users maintain a blog. All those blogs. Something has to be good. Why not yours?

9. Pew Internet goes on to say that 6 percent of the entire U.S. adult population has created a blog . And now we know why nobody answers the phone when we call.

10. According to Sifry, Technorati is currently tracking over 70 million blogs. See number six. Some of them have to be good.

11. Sifry adds that over 120,000 blogs are created every day. This is not posts. This is sites. BM2hosting.com says zoom, zoom . . . as does WordPress . . . and Blogger and . . .

12. There are over 1.4 million new blog posts every day, according to Sifry. What in the world do all these people have to say?

13. Bloggers that update their sites multiple times daily get 2.6 times as many reads as sites with just static pages.

14. Twenty-two of the 100 most popular web sites in the world are blogs. One of mine is #13,000ish. Just 12,900 spots to go!

15. According to *Addage*, 37 percent of blog readers began reading blogs in 2005 or 2006. It's not too late to get in the game.

16. 51 percent of blog readers shop online, says Clickz. What are you selling?

17. Clickz also instructs that blog readers average 23 hours online each week. See number seven. Find more info on these at http://www.blogworldexpo.com/.

And here are five more very good reasons. Technorati says of all bloggers, hobbyists, and professional (that's me!) alike,

---

1. 63 percent of bloggers say "blogging has led them to become more involved with the things they are passionate about." How much fun can it be to write and share about something you have fun doing! Blogging allows me to do that. Blogging can be a great platform for you to do the same.

2. 71 percent of probloggers "have a greater visibility in their industry." You got something to say? Need listeners?

3. 63 percent of probloggers say "clients have purchased their products and services." What are you peddling?

4. 56 percent of probloggers say "they are now regarded as a thought leader." Who is Mario Armando Lavandeira, Jr.? Mario's blog is one of the top 100 most-read sites on the Net. He was asked to be a judge for the Miss USA contest. Because of his pointed question to one contestant and his position on gay rights, that particular contestant lost. He also goes by Perez Hilton.

5. 40 percent of probloggers say "they have been asked to speak at conferences." I have been asked . . . and asked . . . and asked. And quite often I have said yes, and thoroughly enjoyed it! Just two weeks prior to writing this, I was in Malaysia speaking at a publishing convention and a digital media convention.

Still not convinced you should, ought, or might want to blog? Then never mind. You can stop reading now, because the rest of this book won't matter. But please pass this book along to someone who can benefit from it, and maybe they will thank you in their blog!

Following this chapter there will be a test, so read carefully, please.

How do you know if you have what it takes to be a Professional Blogger?

I am a professional blogger. By that I mean that my blogs pay my sizable Silicon Valley mortgage. Revenue from traffic ALONE at my blogs pays my bills. And until my wife got a pretty good job not long ago, blogging was the primary source of income for my wife, my four-year-old, and me. It still might be the main source of our income. I never check those things.

What I want to say is that a problogger pays the bills or maybe just pays one bill with his or her blog. I want to explain what I think the characteristics are that a blogger needs to bring to the table in order to determine whether or not he or she has what it takes to be a problogger.

Before I get going on the personality of the problogger, let me explain the different ways a blog can make money.

---

1. **A blog can make money by selling something that the blogger owns**.

A service, a product, consulting. That sort of thing. You don't need a LOT of traffic for this to happen. Just the right kind. Please read again the testimony of the remodler in the chapter on why blogs are King of social media. The short is that KC used his blog to bring attention to a service he offered. This will also work for authors. Please checke out www.hookedonthe book.com.

2. **A blog can make money by selling something that somebody else owns.**

What happens is that a blog gets traffic. The blog owner searches out an affiliate from the likes of www.ClickBank.com and sells a product or products from there that matches the content of his or her site. My daughter has a site—www.HowILearnedToBe.me. She writes about growing up biculturally and has a link to an affiliate that teaches people how to learn a second language. But you need enough traffic and a good affiliate match to make this work.

3. **A blog can make money by selling ads directly to contacts the blogger has developed.**

I have a client who is an adventurer—www.mrhalfdome.com. He has a great site that gets good traffic about a very specific niche. He has reached out to businesses in his niche and they have purchased ad space on his site. His blog makes him money. If he does it more, he can make enough money to feed his adventure costs and then some.

4. **A blog can make money by getting enough traffic that someone wants to place ads on it**.

That's what I do. I get anywhere from 1.5 to 2 pages viewed per second. Page views are more important to me than visitors because I get paid by how many impressions I generate. The rate per impression might be low, but if I can generate enough impressions, the blog site will work for me. I just need more relevant content.

If your blog has enough traffic, advertisers will solicit you to place their ads. That's what happens to me. How will you know if you have enough traffic? Keep writing till you get an email asking you to place an ad. It is different for each niche.

5. **Any combination of the above.**

Try a combination of one or more of the above and you can make money with and from your blog.

Fred Gleeck has become a good and reliable friend of mine. He is an information marketer extraordinaire. He gives great advice to those starting off in his field of information marketing. The advice is good for those wanting to be probloggers as well. He tells people NOT to be concerned about paying all of their bills with their online business. Rather, he tells them to start off by paying just some of their bills or even one of their bills. Make enough money to buy your coffee for the month. Gas money. It might be cheaper than the coffee. Your cell phone bill. Your car payment. My car lease is cheaper than my cell phone payment. Hmm . . . You get the idea.

Start off with the goal of your blog paying something and before long it'll pay for a lot more.

Do you have what it takes to be a problogger?

Here's what I recommend. Take the test and check your score. Then read through my explanation of each item and how to improve your score and try again based on any new understanding you might have.

And if your score is really low, as much as I love you, try something else. Problogging is not for everyone. But if you still really, really want people to think you are a problogger, contact me and I will find someone to ghost blog for you and you get the byline. Seriously. Contact me at bill@billbelew.com and I'll see what I can do for you.

Test— Are You Blogger Material? (Exercise #2)

5—You betcha!!!!
4—Well, yeah, usually.
3—Yeah, I suppose I do.
2—Hmm, lemme think . . .
1—Nope, not me.

	5	4	3	2	1
Do I enjoy writing?	5	4	3	2	1
Do I have a message?	5	4	3	2	1
Do I like to be the center of attention about my topic?	5	4	3	2	1
Am I a self-starter?	5	4	3	2	1
Do I have self-discipline?	5	4	3	2	1
Can I make a commitment?	5	4	3	2	1
Am I thick-skinned?	5	4	3	2	1
Do I enjoy being in the public spotlight?	5	4	3	2	1
Do I know my way around the back end of the store?	5	4	3	2	1
Do I have a sense of humor?	5	4	3	2	1
Can I balance my ego with humility?	5	4	3	2	1
Do I like to learn?	5	4	3	2	1
Do I enjoy reading?	5	4	3	2	1
Am I an organized person?	5	4	3	2	1
Am I a social person?	5	4	3	2	1
Am I a creative person?	5	4	3	2	1
Do I have perseverance?	5	4	3	2	1
Am I me?	5	4	3	2	1
Am I willing to work hard?	5	4	3	2	1
Do I know when to stop?	5	4	3	2	1

MY TOTAL SCORE _____

Check your score below to see where you stand.

100–81–Show me the blog dashboard = You have what it takes.

80–61–Hold on while I get my coffee = Wait, I thought you wanted to go to work and you're going where?

60–41–I'll be there, I'll be there = Think again.

40–21–Hang on. Lemme finish this program = Never mind. This isn't for you.

20–1–I thought you said Bologna! = You are full of baloney if you think this line of work is for you.

Here are the 20 questions again with an in-depth explanation of what I mean AND what I think bloggers could do to improve themselves to get a better score.

1. Do I Enjoy Writing?

If you don't enjoy writing, don't blog. Blogging is writing, too. It might not be novel writing, memoir writing, or poetry, but it's still writing. I roughly and realistically estimate that I hit my IBM Thinkpad laptop keys more than 20,000,000 times before I saw the first 1 million unique visitors come to my web site. Seriously. That's 20 million times. I know how many words I wrote and multiplied that by an average of seven taps per word plus the space bar. By the time I got to 20 million, they "I" key on my laptop stopped working. You have to enjoy looking at the screen on your PC/Mac a LOT. You have to enjoy the process of punching keys and finding meaning in the combinations you produce. You have to enjoy hitting the publish button and seeing your words on the printed page, um, screen. And if you don't enjoy it, you need to find the motivation to do it from somewhere deeper. I know several deeper sources. Watch the video A Penny A Page to learn the answer.

2. Do I have a Message?

I tell my online students that the reason most people can't write (can't speak, either for that matter) is because they don't have anything to say. Do you have something burning inside your bones? Jeremiah the prophet is one of my favorite characters. He preached gloom and doom for some 40 years. (How fun can that be?) And not a few times he became discouraged. Buried in a pit? That'll do it. Forced to walk the streets in your underwear? That'll surely do it. At one point he even decided to give up. But then, the passion for his message overtook him. When he decided he didn't want to preach any more, the overwhelming desire to continue became like a "fire in his bones," and he said he "grew weary from holding it in." Passion will keep you motivated. It may be the evangelist in me. If I know something good, something cool, I can't help but want to tell people. Sharing the good news is just something I am wired to do. When was the last time you heard/read something really cool and you couldn't wait to tell someone? That's what you want to write about. But there are other motivators. If you didn't or couldn't click through to watch the video above, here's a snippet from a blog post I wrote about this motivator:

Report: Blog workshop held on how to get more traffic and what you can do with it.

At one point during the workshop I touched on the 20 characteristics of a successful blogger.

On that list, near the top, was the word Passion.

I jumped up and down, told the story of Jeremiah the prophet and how he could not not preach because whenever he decided he wouldn't continue, the message of God burned like fire in his bones.

See Jeremiah 20:9.

I was feeling pretty good about myself and that particular point until I read one of the comments in the feedback forms after the presentation.

"How do you get so passionate about cricket? or Bollywood?" I was asked.

Thankfully, I didn't have to answer that on the spot. It got me to thinking about what else might motivate a blogger.

I found in myself the simple answer—hunger.

Even a blogger has to eat, pay the rent, that sort of thing.

When I started blogging more than six years ago, I started it as a vocation. I decided I'd make a living at it or at least pay my mortgage (I do now!) no matter what.

Passion and hunger—two great motivators.

If you don't have a message burning inside you to get out, then make the commitment to live off your blogging, come what may.

Either one of those should keep you motivated.

If not hunger or passion—how do you stay motivated when there is nobody to tell you to write?

I have thought longer and harder about this. And I have learned at least two other motivators that might trump passion and hunger. But not yet. I will write about them later.

3. Do I Like to be the Center of Attention about My Topic?

There are in my mind two kinds of writers. Some writers will write even if nobody ever reads their stuff. Other writers write because they want to get read. I want to get read. Then there are two kinds of writers who write to get read. Those who want to make money for their words and those who don't care if they make any money or not. I want to get read and I want to make money doing it. Legitimately, of course.

A blog is a good way for folk to come find out what you have to say about your subject. That is, they want to hear what you have to say and not somebody else. Are you okay with that? Or do you prefer to be just another voice in a crowd? If so, a forum might be better for you. If you write long enough about your topic, sooner or later people are going to start showing up to find out what you have to say. It just works. I cannot guarantee what a third party will do. By that I mean I cannot guarantee what a search engine will do. But from my experience, if you write enough, on topic enough, with good search engine optimization techniques in your tool bag, you will get found and people will read you.

One of my clients, www.hookedonthebook.com, (mentioned earlier) started updating their content at the beginning of 2012. Within six months they were seeing more than 500 unique visitors each day to their web site about a children's book on the Bible that they had written and illustrated. If you write it, readers will come over time. Are you okay being read?

4. Am I a Self-Starter?

It is easy to start a blog. Not long ago I created a blog for a church. Bought the domain name, got the hosting, installed WordPress, chose a template, created pages . . . about two hours from zero to ready to show people.

It takes character to get visibility to your blog and to keep it going. When I owned my company in Japan, I would hire teachers from overseas. Without exception, they were quite proud of themselves once they showed up in Japan. How hard is that? Get a visa, buy a ticket. Showing up is easy. It's what comes after that that matters. Nobody is likely to ever tell you, "okay, better go post something now." We have nearly 30,000 articles at my network of sites. More than 12,000 times I told myself to go write something. Seriously. I love my wife, but she never ever asked me, "Are you going to write today?" Or, "Did you write something yesterday?" Never ever. I told myself over and over again to go write. And I did. Can you tell yourself to go write? And do you listen?

5. Do I have Self-Discipline?

Not only do you need to tell yourself to write, you also need to tell yourself to be consistent, to stay on topic, use good SEO principles, and stay with it for the long haul. How long? Till your voice catches on. Till you get the results you want. Do you have the self-discipline that is needed to post quality stuff, the right amount of it, often enough, for the duration it takes to catch on?

I can think of two basic approaches to a blog when starting out. Some bloggers will decide they will write as much as they can, work hard at it, give it their very best effort, and see what happens. Other bloggers will decide how much traffic they want and write till that many people show up. Which one are you? I have received as many as 10K visitors in a lifetime to one of my blogs. 10K visitors in a year. 10K visitors in a month. 10K visitors in a day. 10K visitors in an hour. 10K visitors in a minute. 10K visitors in a second . . . not. How many people do you want to show up to your site? And how often? Are you willing to work until that many people show up? Or are you just going to do your best? They are different mindsets, to be sure. I am the latter. And do you have the self-discipline to tell yourself to stay with it till you see the results you want? Not the results you get, but the results you want?

6. Can I make the Time Commitment?

As in life, you pretty much get what you pay for in blogging, too. You put in the time, put up the content, and you will see a return for your effort. When I was in Japan, my students and I participated in yearly walk-a-thons. These consisted of 100 km (62.1 miles) walks. We took pledges, then headed out. Generally speaking, there were two types of walkers. There were those who promised to go as far as they possibly could, to give their all, to walk until their feet hurt beyond imagination and they could go no more, at risk of being unable to work or go to school the next day. Then there were the walkers who pondered out loud, "I wonder how long it will take?" The second bunch had made up their mind they were going to do it and it was just a matter of time. You can well imagine which type of walker was the kind that usually finished the walk.

When I started off as a blogger, I wrote 15–20 articles of about 200 words EACH day. Every day for more than a year before I saw the first 1,000,000 unique visitors to my mini network of three sites. I saw nearly 1.6 million views total from those visitors. It took me around three to four hours each morning to write that much. I was up around 4 a.m. writing. I did this BEFORE I went off to the local college to teach classes. (A guy has to eat while he grows his blog, right?) I wrote those 20 articles BEFORE teaching at the local college in the morning and BEFORE teaching 300+ (count 'em) online students in the afternoon. Really! I wrote and taught that much each day. I was willing to make the time commitment that it took until I saw the level of traffic I wanted. I now get 1,000,000 visitors every one to two weeks and have seen as many as 1 million visitors in three days.

Harry's neighbors could be seen sitting on the roofs of their houses during a major flood. One shouted to the other, "Look at that hat in Harry's front yard!"

> "Yeah, isn't it funny how it's going back and forth, back and forth in straight lines while it moves across the yard?"
> "Nope, not really."
> "Uh, why not?"
> "Well, Harry told me yesterday that today, come hell or high water, he was going to mow his lawn."

Are you willing to make the commitment?

The astute reader has now realize that this characteristic is a key motivator. Beyond passion and hunger there is resolve. Make up your mind you are going to do it or . . . There is nothing that comes after or.

But there is another motivator.

7. Am I Thick-Skinned?

Every writer I have met says they want feedback. That's not really true. What most people really want is for people to say nice things to them. They want "good" feedback. Most people say they want feedback. And that might be true until they start getting comments. What writers are really saying is that they want people to blow smoke up their backside, to tell them they are doing a good job. They want comments so they can share with friends, "This is the reason I write!" Good comments do come but the majority of comments are not so flattering. Maybe I am just a bad writer or perhaps I am just on the wrong side of my topic. That's entirely possible. From my experience readers are more likely to tell me where I am wrong than where I am right. They will tell me when I can't spell. I can. There's a difference between typos and not knowing how to spell. They will tell me when my facts are off and call me stupid. I just go into my dashboard and make the correction. Then they look stupid. They will tell me when I am barking up the wrong tree. I can't help what they think. But I do know what I think and why. I tell people that I don't care whether people love me or hate me (I prefer love nonetheless). I just don't want people to be indifferent to me. But you need to be very thick-skinned to endure many of the comments you will receive. Are you thick-headed, I mean, thick-skinned? All feedback is good, but not all, not even most feedback is positive.

8. Do I Enjoy being in the Public Spotlight?

Once you hit publish, it's out there . . . in cyberspace . . . and folk can read it, quote you, blast you, praise you, report you, and even forward your writing on to others. There is a delete/remove button in blogging, but "takebacks" are almost as hard in the virtual world as they are in the real world. It's fun to be in the public spotlight when it's the popular position. But when you are not in the mainstream position, there is no limit to the cruelty of some. Some of my readers blame my mother for the "stupid" things I write. And she has been dead for several years. That being said, I was interviewed for a position at a local church last year. After interviewing several candidates the church decided to hire me despite the differences in our beliefs—not a small thing considering it was a church. When I asked them why they hired me, they replied, "We read one of your columns about your Christian Worldview. And when we saw where you stood on the tough issues, we knew you were the person we wanted." And my position was NOT in the mainstream. Being in the public spotlight does not bother me. How about you?

9. Do I know My Way Around the Back End of the Store or in this Case, the Dashboard of My Blog Software?

It is not necessary to know how to do everything your blogging software dashboard can do, but if you do know how, things can go a lot smoother . . . or not. Some folk think that when they are tweaking or outright changing the look of their site, they are doing something. They think that when they are installing widgets or adding plug-ins they are doing something. They are. I call it fiddling. They are not writing, putting up content, getting read, hitting publishing, or blogging. The single most important thing a blogger can do is to put up content. Lots of it, regularly over a long period of time. Everything else is everything else. Other things are important, but not as important as writing and hitting publish. That's why a blogger should consider being part of a network. More often than not, the tech support of the network will do all the necessary fiddling and the blogger can write. That is, the blogger can do what he or she does best and is most passionate about . . . write. Still, knowing the basics of the dashboard helps out a LOT. Or bloggers need to know someone they can trust or have the money to pay someone who can do it for them.

10. Do I have a Sense of Humor?

Life is short, take it easy. Life is short, go gung-ho while the going's good. Bloggers must be ready to laugh at themselves. Others will certainly laugh at you and make fun of you as well. You might as well do it yourself. I remember an article I wrote, The ABC's of Evolution. Agree with me or not, I believe there is more than sufficient scientific evidence for a young earth. I know this position is not popular with a lot of very loud folk in the blogosphere. So what? I wrote it anyway. Every atheist and their brother came to yell at me. I welcome you to go there and yell at me too if you disagree. Or, better yet, please go and leave some encouragement. Anyway, the atheists called me every name in the book and accused me of every shortcoming there is. They claimed I was born in a stupid tree, fell out and hit all the stupid branches on the way down, and landed in a stupid puddle. They told all their friends how stupid I was and their friends came and called me AND my mom stupid. She's not even around any more! Comments out the wazoo, most all of them blasting me. And the only thing I could think of was "Ka-ching! Ka-ching!" Every time they came I got paid (paid by the page views). And they made this article more findable so that even more people can come. Thanks, guys! Who's stupid now? No, I don't think they are stupid. Wrong? Yes. Stupid? No. Point is that you have to have a sense of humor. Can you take it when people laugh at you? Can you laugh at yourself?

11. Can I Balance My Ego with Humility?

There's a reason why Jesus said, "The meek will inherit the earth." And in another place, Solomon says, "Pride goes before a fall." It is easy enough to get 150,000 visits in a day or even 500,000 if you stick with it long enough. Okay, it is not really that easy. I explain how to do that in other books, workshops, and at my blog. But does that mean I am the dude? No. More often than not it means I was in the right place at the right time. I wrote about the right thing at the right time. I didn't cause the politician to die or the button to come off someone's blouse or the athlete to do something unprecedented or the test results to come in or . . . I just wrote about it. Thomas Jefferson said, "I find that the harder I work the luckier I am." I am a hard worker. So, I get lucky more often than others. Not because I am great but because I am blessed. No ego here. Just gratefulness that my readers come and come, new people can find me more and more. How about you? Can you find the right balance between ego and humility? After all, it's just a blog.

12. Do I Like to Learn?

Do you think blogging is ONLY about telling readers what you know, think, or what you have learned and know and think about that? Can you still be taught? Or do you just teach? Continued learning keeps the blogger and his or her material fresh. I spent nearly 20 years in Asia. But I do NOT know everything there is to know about Asia. I have earned the privilege of sharing my thoughts on this huge continent but there is still a LOT, a very LOT that I do not know. A good rule of thumb: I spend at least as much time putting stuff in my head—learning—as I do dumping it out—writing at my blog sites. How much time do you spend learning each day? Do you enjoy learning? Is it a struggle to learn? The desire to get new information and share it should be in your DNA. When it is there, you will be a better blogger.

13. Do I Enjoy Reading?

To be a good writer, reading is fundamental. For example, reading other blogs enlightens the blogger as to what readers want to read. Reading a lot doesn't necessarily make a blogger a good writer. Writing a lot does that. I have often been asked how I came up with

12,000 things to write about and still haven't run out. As I mentioned earlier, I write about business in Asia. Each morning I ran through my long list of bookmarked pages—half a dozen newspapers in Japan. Another half dozen in China. Then Korea, Thailand, India, Russia, and Taiwan. I'd read through the sites and open up in a new tab things I thought I could write about and comment on. Before long I'd have 40 + tabs open and my Firefox browser would crash and I'd have to do it again. Then I'd start reading and writing. As long as there is news and I can make a connection between my expertise and blog tagline I will have stuff to read and write about. Warning: Don't think just because you are surfing the web and reading a lot of stuff about your topic that you are blogging. That's reading. Blogging is still putting fingers to keyboard and hitting publish at regular intervals. I'll say it again. Everything else is everything else or in a word, fiddling. Blogging happens when you hit the publish button.

14. Am I an Organized Person?

I can hear my wife laughing over my shoulder. I am not organized, but dang! I wish I were. Emails, comments, reading, writing, networking, handling multiple topics, feeds, going to Meetups, giving Meetups, consulting, fighting with partners who are now ex-partners, making deals, advising, getting shares of companies that have no value just to point them in the right direction, chats . . . It is hard for me to stay organized. The other day I was in eight different time zones at once. I live on the west coast of the United States. I was chatting with my son back east and a fellow blogger in Romania on Skype. In another window, one of my writers in India and another in Indonesia were having a three-way chat about what time it would be GMT if a cricket match were being played in New Zealand. I think I was trying to make a point here but I don't remember what the point is now. The best way I know to get organized is to marry someone who is organized.

15. Am I a Social Person?

I am not . . . but I wish I were. Then again, I have folk I work with in India, Pakistan, Bangladesh, Indonesia, Romania, Israel, Taiwan, Japan, China, the United States, and . . . Okay, well maybe I am a bit social . . . at least in the virtual world. Just because the web is impersonal, it doesn't mean it is not personal. The blogger still needs to make real contact with real people. Send emails to and answer emails from real people. I think Facebook and Twitter and Google+ are a waste of time for the blogger. But I also can see the need to maintain real relationships. Hanging out at workshops, think NewMediaExpo, going to blogger Meetups, going to trade shows, being with other people . . . works. One of the best ways to get noticed in the blogosphere is to ask the person physically next to you if he or she has a blog. And when they do, share info and go home and write about it. Being comfortable and enjoying virtual as well as real relationships is a big plus.

16. Am I a Creative Person?

A blogger doesn't have to be creative, but it helps. If you ask me, everything has to do with everything. I can even tie Michael Jackson to my Christian Worldview site if need be. Being able to relate your topic to what is going on in the real world now makes for a good, make that very good way to get readers to come visit your site and see what you have to say. Here's an example of an article at Christian Worldview Examiner. A key to a good blog is being timely and timeless. Timely is making the connection between your topic and what is going on in the world around you. More on that later.

Here is an example of a post I wrote during a Miss America pageant.

I know Carrie Prejean, but who in the world is Mario Armando Lavandeira, Jr.? < = Title

There are lots of people who know who Carrie Prejean is. But who is Mario Armando Lavandeira, Jr.?

Carrie Prejean is the good Christian girl who answered the question about what she thinks about gay marriage and why but might have lost the title of Miss America because of it. She opposes it, because that is the way she was brought up.

Mario Armando Lavandeira, Jr. is nobody that anybody knows. And his opinion matters to nobody and he loses nothing for what he thinks.

Carrie Prejean has convictions and stands up for them at critical times.

Mario Armando Lavandeira, Jr. is nobody, has no convictions and hides.

Carrie Prejean is identified for who she is.

Mario Armando Lavandeira, Jr. steals for and exploits others.

Carrie Prejean is a role model at the young age of 21.

Nobody wants to be like Mario Armando Lavandeira, Jr.

Carrie Prejean has a future.

Mario Armando Lavandeira, Jr. has no future. He no longer exists.

My hat's off to Carrie Prejean. She has my love and admiration.

Mario Armando Lavandeira, Jr. gets nothing.

Who is Mario Armando Lavandeira? Do a search to find out.

My point is that with just a bit of creativity I could find a way to take a current event and make it relevant to my readers. I have stretched the relevance factor too far at times, made a connection when there really wasn't one just because I knew I could get traffic. If I do this too often, my site will lose focus and eventually ranking in the search engines. Staying on topic is key. Making the connection when it is there is golden. Stretching things too often makes them wear out and break. Are you creative?

17. Do I have Perseverance?

It takes time for a blog to catch on.

Here's an example of perseverance.

Let me tell you a story about my older son (he drew the illustrations for this book).

When Benjamin was seven years old, he and I participated in a biathlon (run-bike-run). We were required to run 5 km (3.1 miles), bike 60 km (37.2 miles), and run another 5 km. We ran the first 5 km and he (seven years old, mind you) wasn't last. We took off on our bikes. I was on my road racer and he was on his one-speed BMX (big problem). We puttered along getting cheers and grins from all sorts of folk including the volunteers who were supposed to tell us when to turn.

> "Go Benji! Isn't he cute?" (referring to me, of course . . . not!) cheered the girls. But nobody told us when to turn (second big problem).

We continued on until we came to a big mountain. Anything uphill is big when you are on a one-speed and are not old enough to have muscles. I realized we were not on the 60 km course, but on the 100 km course (62.1 miles) and we were climbing . . . um, very slowly.

"Benji, we are on the wrong course. Let's turn around."

"No!" Climb, climb, grunt.

"Benji, it's the wrong course. Let's go back."

"Uh-uh." Grunt, grunt, climb.

"Benji, we can't climb this hill. It's too big. Besides, it's the wrong course. Let's coast back down to the right course.

No answer.

Two or three more turns of the pedal and he and his bike fell over.

"Now we can go back."

No answer. Benji righted his bike, grabbed the handlebars, and started pushing his bike up the hill!

I started crying. He started crying. And we both pushed till we crested the large mountain. When we got to the top, Benji said, "Now, we can go back."

That's commitment, perseverance, determination . . . all those good words . . . in a seven-year-old. We finished the course.

Some tell me that I should steer my son away from trying to make a living as an artist.

Are you kidding me? Do you think for one moment I would tell my son what he canNOT do?

Benji now is a world-class pianist, having won international competitions in Japan. He paints fine art and does illustration work, having worked as an animator for a Japanese animation company. He is making a living as an artist.

What's your perseverance level to your blog?

■ 18. Am I Me?

Are you honest, transparent? If you are not being you, who will be you? A blog is your place. Don't worry about being like others, sounding like others. Write in the first, second, or third person. Don't worry about your literary skills or lack of them. I can honestly say with no sense of false humility that I am not a particularly good writer. I know how to write, spell, and use good grammar. As mentioned before, I spent nearly 20 years in Japan where I seldom used more English than, "This is a pen!" I know how to write to please search engines AND real people. I know good search engine optimization techniques. I know the balance. I write like me and nobody else. Be you and be the best you there is.

■ 19. Am I Willing to Work Hard?

Blogging is not hard, it's not easy. It's kind of like learning a language. Wait, that's hard, you say. Well, little kids can learn a language, right? Being a good blogger requires doing relatively easy things over and over and over again until it's done write, um, right. Putting up content is not that hard. It's the "over and over" that's hard. It's dealing with the –sistent family (persistent, consistent, insistent) that's hard. Indeed the hardest part is usually getting to the pool, um keyboard.

I have another son. Story time.

Micah, my second son, was a swimmer through elementary school, junior high, and high school. At one time he and I were living in Buffalo, NY, and anybody who knows anything knows there is snow in Buffalo . . . especially in the winter. He and I got up early (5:00 a.m.)

one morning for a regular practice. I took him to practice in my little front-wheel-drive Toyota Corolla. No easy feat, mind you, considering how much snow there was that winter. And it wasn't the first time either. Because of circumstances, Micah was swimming alone AGAIN, in a 20-yard pool, with a private coach who did NOT show up . . . again! Micah (14-years old) was devastated, looked at me, and said, "I quit."

> "You can do as you please, you know," I said. "But remember you are not the only one who showed up this morning or every other morning, for that matter. It's your call."

(For what it's worth, I have NEVER EVER told my son Micah to swim or Benji to play the piano. I have told them to stop. But not to go.)

Micah went up to the locker room and I packed all the gear up and waited.

Ten, then 20, 30 minutes went by. Far too long to change clothes. And we had to get to school! He then came back out in his swimming suit, looked at the blackboard where I had written his workout, and jumped in the water and started swimming. For two hours straight he swam, only glancing at the blackboard long enough to know what to do next. He swam, turned, swam, turned, glanced, swam, turned. Lots of extra turns because the pool was a short pool. When he was done with the entire workout, he jumped out and climbed the steps to the locker room, saying nothing. Ten minutes later he came out and we went home in silence. Micah became national champion as a freshman in the 200-yard freestyle as a freshman in junior college. He went on to finish his college career at a Division I school on a full-ride swimming scholarship (Can you say six figures?).. After that he finished his master's degree in molecular exercise physiology at a University of California school. He is now in a paid PhD program at UMASS medical school. That's hard work and commitment. Do it or . . . there is nothing that comes after "or." If you're going to blog, then blog. Don't just try to blog. Because if you are just messing around with your blog, all you do is clutter up the blogosphere. It's hard work that anybody can do if they just work hard.

20. Do I Know When to Stop?

This is hard for me. I am stupidly stubborn and at times just plain don't know when to quit. That's good and bad. If a person is stubborn and successful, it is said she or he has done well. If a person is stubborn and fails, he or she is just plain stubborn. Blogging often offers immediate returns. Publish something . . . people come. Publish more . . . more come. A blogger has to know when to turn off the machine, to go into the house, to spend time with family and other real people. If not, blogging can become addictive. I know. You might think that here is a dad who drove his sons mad. Not so. As I said, I never, ever told my older son to practice the piano or the younger one to swim. Ask them. I had to tell them when to take a break. I wish I had been able to show them by example. I wish I could tell myself when to stop. If only I had learned how to use the schedule function in my WordPress blog sooner! A good preacher friend of mine once said in passing, "You can do more work in six days than you can in seven." It was terribly convicting. And I immediately applied the principle. He was right. I learned to work more efficiently and accomplish more in total over six days when I knew I was going to take a complete day off. Know when to stop.

Time for the test. When you are done, email me at bill@billbelew.com (yes, my real email address) and let me know how you did.

Test— Are You Blogger Material? (Exercise #2)

5—You betcha!!!!
4—Well, yeah, usually.
3—Yeah, I suppose I do .
2—Hmm, lemme think . . .
1—Nope, not me.

	5	4	3	2	1
Do I enjoy writing?	5	4	3	2	1
Do I have a message?	5	4	3	2	1
Do I like to be the center of attention about my topic?	5	4	3	2	1
Am I a self-starter?	5	4	3	2	1
Do I have self-discipline?	5	4	3	2	1
Can I make a commitment?	5	4	3	2	1
Am I thick-skinned?	5	4	3	2	1
Do I enjoy being in the public spotlight?	5	4	3	2	1
Do I know my way around the back end of the store?	5	4	3	2	1
Do I have a sense of humor?	5	4	3	2	1
Can I balance my ego with humility?	5	4	3	2	1
Do I like to learn?	5	4	3	2	1
Do I enjoy reading?	5	4	3	2	1
Am I an organized person?	5	4	3	2	1
Am I a social person?	5	4	3	2	1
Am I a creative person?	5	4	3	2	1
Do I have perseverance?	5	4	3	2	1
Am I me?	5	4	3	2	1
Am I willing to work hard?	5	4	3	2	1
Do I know when to stop?	5	4	3	2	1

MY TOTAL SCORE _____

Check your score below to see where you stand.

100–81—Show me the blog dashboard = You have what it takes.

80–61—Hold on while I get my coffee = Wait, I thought you wanted to go to work and you're going where?

60–41—I'll be there, I'll be there = Think again.

40–21—Hang on. Lemme finish this program = Never mind. This isn't for you.

20–1—I thought you said Bologna! = You are full of baloney if you think this line of work is for you.

How did you do?

Got what it takes? If so, I'll see you in the blogosphere. And let me know if I can help out in any way.

CHAPTER 8

21 Characteristics That Define Quality in a Blog

Quality is sometimes a subjective term. What is considered good quality to one person is not necessarily the same to another. One person might like a tune, and another may think, "Huh? You call that music?" Quality in a blog can be defined, however. There are elements that, if included in a blog post, will increase the quality of that post. And the more a blog post has of these elements, the better the quality. WARNING—there are a lot of lists, and lists within lists. Good luck!

Here are 21 characteristics that give quality to a blog.

1. Original Content

There's a reason this needs to be said. There are a lot of blogs that are spam blogs, spam news and the like. They are just repostings of someone else's original content elsewhere. Sometimes a blogger will write one post and put it up at many different sites. Please be sure that the first site to get the original content will win out in the search engines in the long run. Bloggers will want to write their own stuff. Bloggers will not want to copy from someone else or let someone else steal their stuff. It happens a LOT.

2. 200-Word Minimum

This is a universal truth. For news sites to pick up a blog post and for advertisers to get a good feel for what ads to attach (if used), a post needs to be at least 100 words long. That's all? Yup. That's all. More is okay, too. My experience—150–250 words works best. Anything longer than 300 words can be divided into two posts and given part 1 and part 2 in the title. This is great to get readers to return. Blogs are one-minute affairs. Readers don't study blog posts. They read them for information purposes or as discussion starters. There is a place, however, for longer and more involved posts. More on that later. And of course there are exceptions. See www.instapundit.com. He writes short and shorter and it works. But most cannot get away with that style. For me, the 150–250 rule has worked quite well.

3. At Least One Visual Image

Find an image, clip art, or a photo to include in the post. There's an option to title/caption the image and the title should be relevant to the blog post content. If you are writing about Michael Jackson going to church, title the photo/image "Michael Jackson Goes to Church" or something similar.

Where to Find Free Images

Usually the first place I go to find free images is Google Images search (http://images.google .com/).

In some regards, I hate depending on search engine results as much as the next guy, but some search engines do good work. For example, Google Images provides a list of images from everywhere on the web. The blogger needs to be careful to ensure that any image he or she uses from Google Images is not copyrighted (which should be obviously stated in conjunction with the original source of the image). If it's copyrighted, don't use it unless you get permission. This is done by contacting the photographer and asking. Same for Yahoo Images search (images.search.yahoo.com/). Yahoo is useful, too. There are other sites, of course. Search free images. Try www.sxc.hu, www.imageafter.com, wikipedia.com or www.morguefile.com. When using an image found via a search, it is good form to give a link back to the site where it was found. One of the very best ways to do this is to use your own images/photos. Nothing will beat that for you long term. You can also hire an illustrator to create a library of you doing what you do and use the images over and over again and recaption them accordingly to make them suit the content. I use my sone www.benjaminbelew.com.

4. At Least One External Link

More often than not, a blogger might read another blog or a news item or some such source and want to comment on it or make a contribution to the discussion about the topic. It is good form, great form if it's another blogger, to give a link back to the source where you found your information. Two blogs and two links is even better. Three links? Going into overkill. After all, if you started a discussion, wouldn't you want others to refer to you as the instigator? The answer to that question is, "Yes." www.Technorati.com and blogsearch.google.com are great places to start to find other bloggers who may be writing about the same topic as yours. It's a great idea to say your piece and make reference, with a link, to what someone else has said about your topic. After all, don't you like to be quoted? The answer is, "Yes." Here are a few more ideas: Ask.com, IceRocket.com, Blogpulse.com, Blogdigger.com, and Blogcatalog.com. I use Technorati and, well, Technorati is the only one I have every used.

Another good reason to use external links is because this is a way for the search engine to 'see' that your site connects well with a similar site that is on topic . . . creating a mini-web of sorts. That makes for good search engine juju.

5. At Least One Internal Link

An internal link is when you link to something else that you have written. I write about the evolution/creation discussion. Whenever I write something new about the topic, I link to something else I said about it (e.g., in my previous post, "The Evolution Carnival Under the Boardwalk" [hyperlinked], I said, "Blah, blah . . . blog."). If people are interested in what they are reading they are quite likely to click through to the other post. This will increase your page views. Generally speaking, the more links you have pointing at your site from other sites, pointing to within your site (that is, you referring to your own posts), the better. At least one. Two is good. Three? Back into overkill. It is especially good form to have backlinks from a variety of high-authority sites (see #5).

6. Backlinks from Authoritative Sites

A backlink or trackback is when someone else has linked to your site in his or her article or post. When you link to others, they will link to you . . . sorta. People aren't as polite as they used to be. But that doesn't mean we can't be polite, does it? Search engine creators (Google, Bing, Yahoo, etc.) are always making their algorithms more complicated to thwart spammers.

But links to and from a site are, and likely always will be, a critical part of the search engine ranking formulas. Links, internal and external, are essential for a blog. Besides, people are a curious lot for the most part and they will follow links you provide. The more links your blog has the better . . . to a point. You don't want a blog post that is nothing but links. But then there are sites that have nothing but links—www.popurls.com is one and it gets a lot of traffic.

7. Has Authority

See number six above. The more other blogs in the blogosphere that link to your blog, the better. The more those blogs that link to your blog have blogs that link to them with lots of sites linking to them . . . yaaawwnn . . . the better. Suppose blogger A has 550 people that link to his site. And blogger B has three blogs that link to her site. Both write about the same topic as you. Technorati will tell you how many blogs there are that link to his, her, or your site. Which blog, A or B, will you hope notices your site and links to it? B . . . not! A, of course. The blogger will want to be sure that his or her blog is claimed by Technorati. Technorati has instructions for this, or your blog network tech support can do it for you. Incidentally, it should be further evident at this juncture why it is advantageous to belong to a blog network. I will say again that there is instant link love if a blog network will have you. You get the power of links from other blogs in the network, and they from you. Of course, you are making out much better than the blog network.

8. Adds Something Unique

By virtue of the fact that I lived in Asia for nearly 20 years, I feel I have somewhat earned the privilege of commenting on many things Asian. Someone may be writing about family relationships in Japan. I do know something about that. I even know what does NOT work. The more your blog post can add that few others or even no other can add, the better the quality of that post. At some point bloggers would want to think that when topic A comes up, people will come to their blog to see what they have to say about the topic.

9. Is About Something People Want to Know

There might be someone who wants to know who has the world record for housing the most vacuum cleaners. That's not me. Chances are if you want to know a lot about a subject, there are other people who want to know as well. These days even niches are huge. I know of a guy that drives around the country doing tailgate parties at football games. He has a huge following, as in tens of thousands of readers daily. Make sure you are the go-to place on your topic.

10. Makes a Contribution to the Discussion

Not long ago there was a big earthquake on the backside of Japan. There were seven nuclear power plants that were shaken and threatened bakin' near the epicenter of that earthquake. I taught English to the engineers who built those nuclear power plants. I drove those streets weekly to teach my classes. When the world was thinking Japan was going to burn in a nuclear bucket, I had a different perspective because I KNEW the area firsthand. My blog about Japan was a great forum for me to add something to that discussion.

◼ 11. Has a Great Title

Clever titles aren't very clever. They are only cute if you have thousands of readers who are subscribed to your site and will get a link to your article via email or their news reader. But search engines don't do clever. Search engines want keyword-specific titles that directly correlate to the content of the blog. The first few lines will restate the keywords of the title in some fashion to reinforce the title. At the end of this chapter is a pretty extensive list of good title patterns. Just insert the keywords that fit your topic. Lots of ideas.

Consider these nine characteristics of a super blog post title:

The Title

1. Clearly states a benefit to the reader. The title promises to meet a specific need.
2. Is descriptive. Simple is good, long is okay as long as the title can be connected to your tagline and is descriptive of the content. Titles longer than 60 characters will get cut off in search engine results.
3. Contains relevant keywords and phrases. A keyword is what the article is about. Make sure there is a connection between the title and the content of your post, otherwise search engines and searchbots get confused (and confused rhymes with fused or fuses, which blow.) You don't want to have a title about cricket streaming and write about the different shades of green balloons for birthday parties just to get hits.
4. Makes a promise to the reader. Readers will get their wishes fulfilled, their dreams will come true, and life will be lived happily ever after . . . or not.
5. Speaks directly but doesn't shout "BUY NOW!!!"
6. Is honest. Sensational works, as does off-topic, but in the end your readers aren't likely to come back unless your blog titles are always honest. Double entendres work but not always. Come to think of it, I think that would make a great blog subject . . . a blog filled with titles that are all double entendres. Hmm . . . doubleentendre.net is available.
7. Uses statistics and numbers, for example, "10 Ways to Lose Weight Fast."
8. Mentions hot topics and famous people. Whenever possible, and it doesn't irritate the dickens out of your personal character, it works to relate a buzz topic or a celebrity to your topic.
9. Appeals to emotional triggers—curiosity, fear, pain, pride, or anger, for example, "The 3 ____ That Will Make Your Co-Workers Envy You."

These nine tips were pilfered from an internal blog at a now-defunct blog network where I used to write. Credit goes to KnowMoreMedia.

◼ 12. Never Runs Out of Ideas

Despite having written more than 12,000 posts I have yet to run out of things to write about. I have a friend who wrote a post—"111 Instant Blog Post Ideas." Insert that title into a search engine and you might still find it at BlogChalkTalk.

Here's another list of ideas (also "borrowed" from the aforementioned internal blog):

- "How-To" posts
- Tips, recommendations
- Your expert advice and opinions on any related topic
- Industry terms/definitions/vocabulary
- The history of your blog topic

- Current events
- Your opinion of a related webpage/blog with link
- Advantage/disadvantages
- Warnings, cautions, concerns
- Reviews/summaries of top providers/related companies
- Reviews/summaries of associations/governing bodies
- Reviews of top authors/journalists
- Product reviews (software, hardware, books, guides, service offerings, etc.)
- New product announcements/reviews
- Reviews/reports on conferences
- Upcoming conferences
- Training/training courses, both online and traditional
- Schools/universities, degrees, and classes
- Continuing education
- Certifications
- Careers/jobs
- Skills needed for success
- Contract/freelance opportunities
- Your own editorial/essay
- Interview with an industry expert and provide the transcript (Q & A style) over several posts
- "Link of the Week" (or "Link of the Day"): a link to a favorite webpage/blog
- Host a poll
- Run a contest
- Jokes
- Anecdotes
- Podcast interviews
- Vidcast interviews

13. Timely

There are any number of ways to find out what people are searching for or reading about on the web in real time. CNN has a list of top news, as does Google and Yahoo. Try Wikipedia Current Events. Try putting a couple of key ideas that pertain to your blog topic into a news alert. Every time it shows up in the news you will get an email that can serve as a prompt of something to write about.

To predict what people might be interested in reading try the likes of http://www. nytimes. com/learning/general/onthisday/index.html

On such and such a date something happened and it will be remembered and/or celebrated. You can tell readers what you remember or what you think needs to be remembered or ask them what they remember. Where were they when Armstrong stepped on the moon, JFK was shot, or Princess Di was killed? I remember where I was.

The University of North Carolina lists the seven basic news values as follows:

Impact: How many people's lives will be affected or influenced in some way by the subject of the story?

Timeliness: Stories that are more current generally have a higher value than those that do not. Journalists often compete for first publication bragging rights for timely stories and exclusives.

Prominence: Prominent public figures and/or officials also have a higher priority than a person who is relatively unknown.

Proximity: Local news almost always (emphasis on almost) has higher news value than something taking place far away.

Uniqueness: Odd news is definitely newsworthy.

Conflict: This one speaks for itself. War, civil strife, and other such occurrences are always newsworthy. If it bleeds it leads.

Currency: This may seem the same as timeliness but it is slightly different. Sometimes issues reappear in the spotlight and there may be some new element of the story worth covering. Think about the follow-up to the death of a celebrity, the fallout because of a merger, that sort of thing.

■ 14. Can Attract Repeat Traffic

Consider these 11 tips on how to get more repeat traffic:

Watch for spikes. Check your sitemeter stats or whatever traffic tracker you are using at least once daily. I do it far too often, but I rarely miss a spike.

Welcome the spikers. If the spike is to your home page, quickly publish a new post that welcomes the readers coming from the source of the spike. I used to get a lot of surges from CollegeHumor, for example. When I knew they were coming, I'd put in a note, "If you found this post/blog in today's CollegeHumor, welcome! Here's what this blog is about and why I hope you'll come back regularly or even sign up for an email subscription." If the spike is coming to a specific blog post, you can do the same by adding a welcome message at the top of the existing post or even at the bottom.

Show them where to go. At the end of all blog posts, consider adding a "Related Links" area where you share three to five articles they might also find interesting. There's a widget that can do this automatically. But it works better if you put a related post within the article.

Give them extra treats. Consider adding something extra to a spiked post—for example, turn a list of 10 tips into 15 or 20 but put the extra information in a brand-new post and ask visitors to click through for more on the topic. "Want more? Read on for part two."

Thank them for coming. You like to be appreciated. So do I. So do our readers. "Hang on! Before you go—I wanted to thank you for coming." Or words to that effect.

Ask them to come back. Did you think of this? Readers like to be invited to do things. Think about inviting them to subscribe to your feed or bookmark your site so they can return daily for the latest news and advice on your topic.

Promise more. Tell readers what you have coming up. Provide a tease. Say something like, "Liked this article? You'll love tomorrow's post. And don't miss next week's post series on a related topic."

Give readers what they want. If one post worked well, give your readers more of the same type of post that won their hearts in the first place.

Write for fanatics. Who do you want to attract to your blog? Write posts that attract die-hards again and again.

Act quickly. Every minute counts when you get a flood of incoming traffic—the faster you take advantage of it, the better.

Prepare for future spikes. Why not prepare in advance a basic welcome message that you can tailor quickly for future spikes? That way, when a spike hits your blog, you are ready.

 ## 15. Engages the Readers (Solicits Comments)

Following is a baker's dozen of ways to encourage people to make comments on your posts:

1. Ask. Do this at the end of your posts. "What do you think about . . .?" or "Do you agree with . . .?" or "Have you ever . . .?" Ask questions that people can't help but want to answer.
2. Encourage people to talk about themselves. "Has this ever happened to you?" "Where were you when . . .?"
3. Make it clear that you welcome and respect all opinions. Let people feel that they are on equal footing with you. Your site allows and encourages differing opinions from your own.
4. Respond quickly to people's comments. Write a reply comment the same day, if possible—the same hour, if you can. And if there is an email address, you can write to your reader directly.
5. Make comments that encourage more conversation. When responding to a commenter, ask a follow-up question. Incidentally, this kind of give-and-take can work well in blog posts. I write a Christian site and I engage regularly with a Jewish writer (on very friendly terms), and we are able to send readers to each other.
6. Pay close attention to the posts that get the most comments. Ask yourself if you should write more posts of the ilk that get comments or something else.
7. Leave your post open-ended. End with a question, for example. Or address one part of an issue, leave the other side untouched, and ask readers to provide the other side.
8. Try to get people to think about what you've said. If you are not interested in your post, your readers won't be either.
9. Let people know that you appreciate their comments. Email a commenter and say thanks. I have on occasion elevated a comment to a post (giving credit) and followed up with my own opinion of the comments.
10. Ask questions. Go beyond "Do you agree?" by asking a question. "I think these are the top five cricket players. Who am I missing and why do you think so?"
11. Stir the pot. People love controversy.
12. Ping other bloggers. Ask bloggers that you respect to comment on something you have written. Who knows, maybe they'll think enough of it to mention it in one of their posts at their own blog site.
13. Leave comments at other blogs. When you leave a comment, you can most often leave a URL to your own site. It is good form when you leave a comment at another person's blogs for them to do the same for you. People do NOT always follow good form, however.

Also, you might want to consider these five reasons why blog comments can be good for your blog:

1. Commenters can become guest bloggers. It's happened for me not a few times.
2. Comments enhance the value and authority of your blog. Many people judge a blog in part by the number of comments it typically receives. I write about Creation. The evolutionists enjoy pounding on anything I say and even send their friends to come harass me as well.
3. Commenters help build relationships. I have virtual friends from all over the world that I met through my comments. I have stayed in the home of a person I met in my

comments. My second trip to Blog World Expo in Las Vegas was free. The network paid for my entrance fee and the commenter put me up in his house. You can't beat that with a stick.

4. Lots of comments can increase traffic and backlinks. People love to refer others to a good conversation. See #2 above.

5. Comments can generate ideas for future blog posts. Indeed, I do get ideas for my articles from my commenters!

But by all means, watch out for trolls! After all that good stuff I just wrote about getting comments at your blogs, I also have to mention trolls. There are people who go about commenting on blogs just for the sake of picking a fight. And you can't tell who is serious and who is not. I have people with names of household fixtures who leave comments at my sites. As a rule, I don't engage with commenters who have not identified themselves. My time is better spent putting up content and encouraging discussion among the commenters that I know are real people.

16. Pillar Content

Pillar traffic breaks the rules of 150–250-word posts. A pillar post is something that readers will come back to again and again, that others can't help but link to. They are also called anchor posts, evergreen posts and linkbait. I wrote a post—21 must-know facts about India + map. I wrote it well over two years ago, yet it gets some 300–400 visits a day. That's a pillar post. I did 12 must-know facts about the Great Wall of China, 15 facts about Asia . . . and so on. Now if I could just write about 100 or even 1000 of those and get the same traffic for each, I'd be in business.

17. Can Go Viral

Viral = virus = bugs = everybody gets them at some time or another. A post that catches on is said to have gone viral. Here are 37 viral post ideas from http://www.skelliewag.org/37-viral-post-ideas-you-can-use-today-103.htm that was written more than 5 years ago. That's good stuff . . . see number 16!

---

1 Assemble one-sentence/paragraph answers to a question you ask key figures across your niche.

2 Create a time spectacle: Create content nonstop over a designated period of time (8 hours, 24 hours?).

3 Write a review of the redesign of a popular blog/website in your niche. Everyone has an opinion on redesigns and will appreciate someone laying out some of his or her own thoughts.

4 Assemble a directory of great interviews conducted with prominent/interesting figures in your niche.

5 Construct a central hub of posts written on a specific, focused topic of great importance to your niche.

6 Create a ranked list of products, services, people, or some other variable within your niche.

7 Offer a free service to everyone who asks, utilizing one of your skills. Then expect nothing in return.

8 Write a history of your niche's presence online. What have been its earliest blogs and websites? Its most popular? Are they still around?

9 Begin a group writing project.

10 Assemble a directory of tips on a topic, delivered in the form of quotes from other sites in your niche.

11 Build a quiz for readers to test their niche knowledge.

12 Offer to write a guest post for anyone who asks. View it as a long-term commitment: Could you manage one guest post a week? The task only becomes insurmountable if you want them all done at once. People will be patient if the service has no strings attached.

13 Conduct two short interviews, both containing the same questions, with two prominent figures in your niche and display the answers side-by-side, allowing us to compare the answers.

14 Assemble a large number of one-sentence tips on a specific topic.

15 Disneyize some key personalities in your niche.

16 Assemble the most interesting or thought-provoking quotes that apply to your niche, even if the person quoted was not talking about your niche specifically.

17 Ask readers a question and have them answer it on their blog/website. Then link to the collected answers from a central hub post.

18 Write a post carefully arguing a view that you feel many of your readers will agree with.

19 Take reader questions and answer them in one post. These can be questions about you, your niche, or your site. Set boundaries if necessary.

20 Link to online tools, software, and sites any person taking part in your niche should know about.

21 Organize an initiative and get other bloggers involved.

22 Take a birds-eye view of your niche; analyze its strengths and weaknesses.

23 Predict what your niche will look like in 5, 10, or 50 years.

24 Create a list of feeds you believe everyone interested in your topic should be subscribed to.

25 Answer a question many of your readers may have, but have not asked because of its complex nature. Some questions of that nature that might be unspoken by readers in this niche, for example, are: What do I do if my blog isn't growing as I hoped it would? How long will it take my site to start generating a worthwhile income? Is there ever going to be a big enough audience for a site in my niche?

26 Address a general "want" shared by most readers in your niche. What are the key three things readers of your site want? For this site, that might be: more traffic, more links, more subscribers. To address the want for more subscribers, I might write a post called: "Ten Innovative Ways to Get More Subscribers." There have been plenty of posts on this subject, but readers are likely to have a look just in case there's something they haven't seen before. To make sure they're rewarded, make certain you meet this need in an innovative/different way.

27 The web is on a productivity/uncluttering trip at the moment. Can you write a guide to being more efficient or productive in your niche? Can you write a guide to getting organized in your niche?

28 Visualize useful information and make it easy to share.

29 Show readers how to construct a cheap object that will prove useful to them.

30 Release a free ebook, packed with value.

31 Write a post answering five important questions, then ask others to answer the same questions on their own sites, promising to link to the answers from a central hub post. Follow through on that promise.

32 Take a famous/interesting person and ask: What approach would that person take to my niche? For example: *The Leonardo da Vinci Guide to Cooking*.

33 Create a ranked list of must-read books relating to your niche.

34 Create a beginner's tour of your topic. If you were showing a beginner the sights, what essential articles should he or she read to get a grip on your niche?

35 Explore what you would change about your niche if you could. What are its short-comings?

36 If you could only share 10 more tips with your readers, what would they be?

37 Assemble a collection of amazing photos/images relating to your niche (some niches will be more suited to this than others).

A viral post is cool. Your site gets a lot of traffic in a short amount of time. But . . . all those visitors will leave and generally not come back. Now if you can get a pillar post to go viral, you might really have something. Especially if you can continue to follow it up. I wrote a post—"20 Hilarious Ratings of Professors at RateMyProfessors.com." It went viral. Some 30,000 people showed up. That was fun. But then where'd they go after that? Who knows?

18. Encourages Subscribers

Subscribers are great. This is better than having an email list except you can't be quite sure who is opening and who isn't. But it doesn't cost anything and the reader manages it.

Here are five ways to get more people to subscribe to your posts AND to get subscribers to give you more blog traffic:

1. Ask. Ask your readers. "If you liked this article, please consider subscribing." Be genuine. But ask.

2. Anticipate. Tell them what they'll miss if they don't come back. Tell them what they can look forward to and why they ought to subscribe now so they don't miss it.

3. Help. Put the button right in front of them. Make it easy for them to subscribe. Tell them how.

4. Thank. Say thanks to your subscribers regularly. Isn't it nice of them to subscribe to your content? Thank them and they're likely to stay.

5. Link. Link out to other blogs so they come running to see what you've got to offer. Link to your own old posts. Plus, email subscribers love clicking on links.

Here's a blog post I wrote about this a long time ago (with a few minor changes to bring it up to date):

5 Reasons to Subscribe to My Blog

This is a shameless plug for this blog. A pitch. A plea. A petition. I genuinely appreciate those who have taken the time to bookmark and/or subscribe to my blog. Thank you very much. As for me, I can think of a few reasons why someone might want to subscribe, some reasons why regular subscribers would introduce this blog to a friend.

1. 11,343,711 and counting reasons. That's how many pages have been viewed at this blog. What's everybody looking at?

2. 5,770 posts. That's how many posts I have written here at this site. There has to be something interesting in there somewhere. Point of interest—my best post here has received more than 100,000 page views. In fact, I have two posts with more than 50,000 page views and 150 with more than 10,000. Almost 200 of them have been viewed at least 1,000 times each. What's everyone looking at? Ask me, and I'll gladly tell you.

3. 6,370 RSS subscribers to date. Those subscribers have to have found something interesting to read. See number two. Maybe you will be interested, too.

4. I read through about 20–30 sites each morning looking for something that I think is interesting and relates to this blog, a lesson learned or something to put in my knowledge pack. Maybe you will be interested, too. Maybe you, the reader, will wonder why I would think the point is interesting.

5. I care about what I write, what I think. And I hope that is reflected in my posts. The things I write about, I do genuinely care about. What do you care about? Are we the same? Are we different? Why do you think so?

How do you subscribe to this blog? It's easy. Just click on the link Subscribe to Bill Belew. Respond. Call me on the carpet. Make me do a better job. Ask me if it's the best I can come up with. Tell me if I did something wrong . . . or right. But consider subscribing. And invite a friend to do so also. Do it today. Do it now. Subscribe to BillBelew.

19. Has Guests, Interviews

Guests and interviews are great for creating links - external, internal and back links. When someone who has a site writes on your site, chances are they will tell their regular readers that they are guest blogging over at your site. This will encourage readers to click through to your site. The guest can leave a link or two in their guest post that will encourage your readers to go to their site to take a look. That's good mojo all around.

Question: So, how do you ask?

Answer: A simple email, a phone call, a comment on their blog—those are common ways.

Following are seven keys to good guest blog recruiting:

- Introduce yourself and your blog.
- Extend the invitation to guest post on your blog.
- Identify a specific topic you would like someone to guest blog about.
- Assure that you'll give clear author credit to the guest blogger, as well as a link to his or her blog/website.
- Give a timeframe for this guest post, but extend an open-ended invitation so they know you'd appreciate their guest posting at any time.
- Provide easy instructions for them to deliver the guest post content to you.
- Explain why you value or admire this person—the reason you're asking him or her to guest blog.

20. Is Attractive to the Social Networks

Here are some social media sites you can submit your posts to:

- StumbleUpon.com
- Del.icio.us, Digg.com
- Newsvine.com
- Fark. com
- Reddit.com
- Shoutwire.com
- Lipstick.com
- IndianPad.com, and, of course, the biggies—Facebook, LinkedIn, Twitter, and Google+.

I have received tens of thousands of visitors and views via this method.

My take on social networks is that they are indeed good for getting traffic. However, I did extensive study on this on my own. I recorded how much time I spent working the social networks, submitting my stuff, getting it submitted, reading others' stuff, and watching the increase in traffic. Indeed, I saw an increase in traffic, but it wasn't worth it in two regards. First, the people came, read, and left and weren't likely to come back unless I worked the network some more. Second, the increase in traffic didn't relate to an increase in income. I spent a lot of time to see more people come who didn't stick, click, and in the end pay for my effort. It just isn't worth it to work the networks, if all you want is more traffic. A blogger is better off in the long run interacting with other like-minded bloggers at their blog sites, via comments and email or even in person, than to work the social media sites.

■ 21. Has a Long Tail

One of the very best posts a blogger can write is a pillar post that goes viral over all the social media sites. If it is good, it will get linked to in a lot of places, making that particular post very findable in the search engines. Remember my 21 must-know facts about India + map. The initial spike that comes can be big. But the traffic that follows coming to that post over the long haul will be greater than the initial spike. That's the long tail. Every blogger hopes for a huge spike of a pillar post followed by a long tail. I have several thousand posts that have more than a thousand visits each. Not many of those posts got a thousand visits initially. They have just been around for a long time and keep getting found over and over again. That's the type of post a blogger wants to write.

Whew! I knew this chapter was going to be long and I did not disappoint myself. But after all, the heart of blogging is putting up good stuff, and these 21 elements define what is good, what is quality, what is the right stuff when it comes to blogs and blog posts. I'd like to say here again that not a few ideas were gleaned from my involvement with KnowMoreMedia. Thanks go to Dan, Easton, and Kimberly for some of these points.

Write more and write well but by all means get blogging!

More Blog Post Ideas —Exercise 3

Choose from this list of blog title starters and use the lines to create your very own. (Hint: This list has endless possibilities!)

What do ___, ___, and ___ have in common?

_____

Can you pass this ___ Test?

_____

Top 10 Tips on ___

_____

Don't Buy the New ___—Here's 5 Reasons Why

_____

How Oprah Does Her Laundry: Secrets Revealed

_____

Who Else Wants [blank]?

_____

The Secret of [blank]

_____

Here Is a Method That Is Helping [blank] to [blank]

_____

Little-Known Ways to [blank]

_____

Get Rid of [problem] Once and for All

_____

Here's a Quick Way to [solve a problem]

_____

Now You Can Have [something desirable] [great circumstance]

_____

[Do something] like [world-class example]

_____

Have a [or] Build a [blank] You Can Be Proud Of

_____

What Everybody Ought to Know About [blank]

_____

Give Me [short time period] and I'll Give You [blank].

_____

If You Don't [blank] Now, You'll Hate Yourself Later

_____

The Lazy [blank's] Way to [blank]

_____

Do You Recognize the [number] Early Warning Signs of [blank]?

_____

See How Easily You Can [desirable result]

_____

You Don't Have to Be [something challenging] to Be [desired result]

_____

Do You Make These [types of] Mistakes?

_____

How to [Mundane Task] That [Rewarding Benefit]

_____

How to

_____

How

_____

How I

_____

What You Should Know About

_____

Do You Recognize/Know

_____

10 Ways to

_____

[Number] Types of [Category of People]—Which Group Are You In?

_____

CHAPTER 9   How Much and How Long?

It is in this last chapter that I feel I have something to offer the world of blogging that nobody else has or knows, or at least I have not seen any study such as the one I have done on the web or anywhere else in print. I have not read anybody else's thoughts on what I want to share here either. Indeed I, too, did not start out to learn the answers to the questions of how much and how long, when I started blogging. But I know the answers now.

The prophets of old often petitioned God when the people were oppressed or when life seemed unfair. Jeremiah asked God, "How long will the wicked prosper?" He wanted to know how long the bad guys were going to have their way while the good guys suffered. John in the Book of Revelation asked God, "How long?" before God would be fair in His judgments.

One fellow might say he has been working very hard to find a job. When asked how much effort he put into his job search, he might reply that he has sent out 20–25 resumes. Another fellow might say that he had sent out more than 600. That's how many resumes I sent out before I got a nibble on a job after moving to Silicon Valley right after the dot-com bust. Bad timing.

How much work do I need to put into my blog? How long do I need to do it before I can see reasonable results? These are great questions. And for the most part the answers may escape us. Not me. I know the answers. I know what has worked for me.

At one stage in my blogging career, I was recording how many visitors I had at each of my blogs at various intervals throughout the day (three hours apart and six times a day) so that I could predict what the traffic would be. Rightly or wrongly, I was placing value on myself and my blogs by how many people came. And for me, more was better. I knew at what pace I was writing, and I watched the traffic far too much. I knew or at least at the time thought I was wasting my time being so obsessed with the figures, but I couldn't not do it. Even now, I have an Excel spreadsheet that goes across the page to GR or some other such two-letter designation. I have a LOT of data, by the day, for every one of my sites.

When the blog network that I belonged to fell out of love with the search engines and the traffic stopped coming via the search engine results, I could pinpoint to the minute when that happened. I knew the numbers behind my sites and the network well enough to do so.

I knew after how many blog posts and at what pace (how many posts per day/week) about what kind of traffic I was getting, and in turn I also learned, after looking at the pattern of several sites, how much traffic I could predict would come if I worked at a certain pace. If I applied the standards outlined in this book, over time I knew what to expect and pretty much when.

Following are screen shots of three sitemeters. The first is PanAsianBiz. The second is RisingSunOfNihon and the third is TheBizOfKnowledge.

PanAsianBiz was created first. In the 10th month, notice what happened to the traffic.

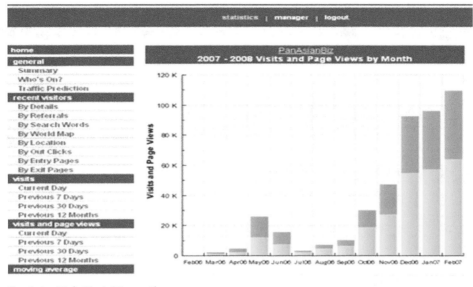

PanAsianBiz's First 10 months

RisingSunOfNihon was created second. Look what happened in the seventh month.

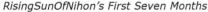

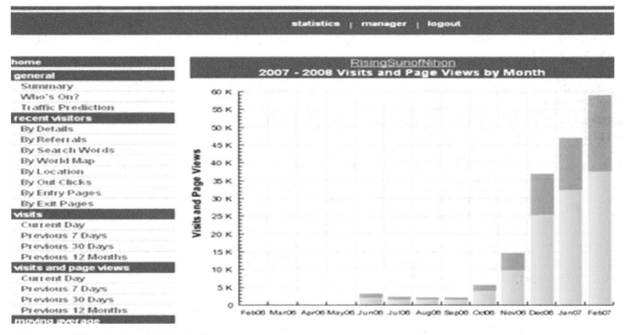

RisingSunOfNihon's First Seven Months

TheBizOfKnowlege came third. Again, can you see what happened in the sixth month?

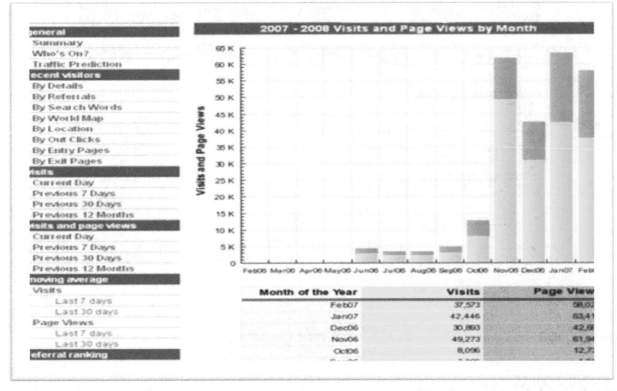

The BizOfKnowledge's First Six Months

After 10 months, 7 months, and 6 months, respectively, the traffic jumped. Leaped! What happened? Why?

At each of the three sites, I wrote at a pace of five posts each day, every day. Every, every day. Thank God for schedulers! I wrote posts in advance and scheduled them to go out on weekends and other days so I could pry myself away from my dashboard. But not my sitemeters! I still checked them faithfully.

The simple conclusion to the how much and how long of blogging:

If a blogger writes the quality-type posts explained previously and works the networks, commenting and such as I explained earlier, the blogger can expect his or her blogs to start growing organically after about 10 months. Organic means there is enough content and the site is vibrant enough that the search engines will notice it more readily and bring more traffic. A second blog will grow faster because it has the benefit of the first blog. A third blog might grow faster because I am smarter . . . in theory, of course.

My answers—a blogger should make it his or her goal to write five posts a day, every day, for about six to nine months (about 1,000 posts total). After which that blogger can expect to see on average 1,000–2,000 visits a day at the site, if not more.

I have subsequently applied this strategy to other blogs, and sure enough the traffic came, and it will work for you.

Take a look at the sitemeter of one of my students.

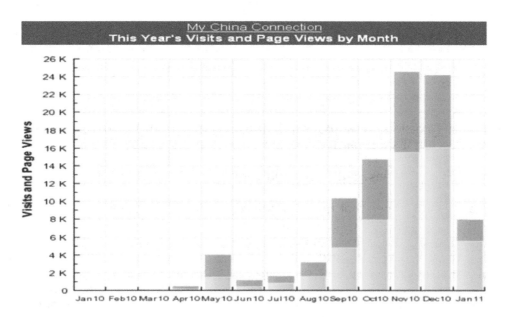

I often get asked, "What happened in January?" I took the screen shot early in January. The trend continued to rise.

BOTTOM LINE—Stick with your blog until it catches on.

Conclusion - It's Not Easy, It's Not Hard

If a blogger wants to have several thousand visitors coming to his or her site daily, the plan is here. It's not easy, but it's not hard.

The hard part is doing the easy stuff over and over again till it catches on.

I have a pair of running shoes that have names. The left shoe is called "Crush it." The right shoe is called "Bag it." The names come from a story written by John Parker of *Once a Runner* fame. He tells about a time when he and some others were working at cleaning up the side of a highway. The trash was everywhere. For all intents and purposes, it was overwhelming. He picked up garbage with one of those little trigger hands with a grabber on the end and tossed it into a plastic garbage bag he held in the other hand. Instead of thinking about the monumental task ahead of him, he just started crushing cans and picking them up one at a time and dropping them in his bag. Crush it, bag it, crush it, bag it. One bag filled up, then another. Rinse and repeat. After a time, the highway shoulder was clean.

I have run 100 miles in a day in 23 hours and 40 minutes. Getting under 24 hours was the goal. That's a lot of running, and 100 miles is pretty far. But given the distance and a day's time I could complete it. When it got hard, I told my left shoe to crush it and my right shoe to bag it, and just kept at it until I was done—the 100 miles were finished.

Friends asked me what I thought about when I ran 100 miles. "Don't you get bored?" The answer is a resounding, "Yes, I got bored." What I thought about was, "Don't think." I just kept putting one foot in front of the other—crush it, bag it—until I was done. If I thought about it, the thoughts that came to mind were, "the distance is too far, I am too tired, I am too sore, I won't be able to work tomorrow," and so on." I could think of every reason in the world why I should have stopped. However, I preferred not to think. I told myself I would think about it when I was done. I had made a commitment to complete the distance. That's all that mattered.

Blogging is not that hard. Make a commitment to putting up about 1,000 posts within the next 6, 9, 12 months. Then put your head down and write. Write (crush it), publish (bag it). Rinse and repeat. And keep at it. Within a year you will have several thousand people coming to your site daily. The formula worked for me again, and again, and again, and again, and again, and again, and again. It WILL work for you, too.

Please write to me a year from now and once you have reached your goal, and dinner will be on me.

My sites have since achieved these two milestones:

10,000+ views in one minute.

500,000 views in one day

And yours can, too.

When they do, let me know. I look forward to hearing from you.

"Bill"

Epilogue

I alluded several times to motivators. What can drive a blogger when passion goes dim.

Hunger is one motivator. If you are bent on feeding your family, you will find a way to stay on track.

Resolve is exceedingly strong. No other option is even considered. To accomplish the task is all there is.

This short story might illustrate the last motivator.

Bumblebees

"Whether you think you can or think you can't, you're right." These words are attributed to Henry Ford, the automaker.

My dad had another way of putting it. "Bumblebees can't fly," he always said. "Their wings are too small and their bodies are too big. The laws of physics are clear... they can't fly," he said. "But they don't know that. So, they fly anyway. If you think you can do something, you can."

Never say can't is what he meant. Where there's a will there's a way. It was that sort of thing.

Benjamin wanted to be a scientist but gave it up to pursue a career in the performing arts instead. Among other pieces, he plays Rimsky-Korsakov's "The Flight of the Bumblebee." I think he does that for a reason.

Benjamin also does as he pleases. After playing the piano for nearly 12 years, he suddenly gave it up along with his piano scholarship to pursue life as an animator. It didn't matter much what advice he was given to the contrary, nor who gave him the advice. He didn't listen to me, his father. He paid little attention to his teachers. His friends proved unreliable confidants. Instead, he listened to the little voice inside that said, "You can do what you put your mind to." After all, it was his life and he was determined to do as he pleased. This is not the same as only trying to please himself. He was going to follow his dream, perhaps fly like a bumblebee.

Benjamin taught himself and in the end successfully passed interviews, screenings, portfolio submissions and tests to get accepted as a 'tweener' (The person who draws all the pictures that hold key animation ideas together) for a large Japanese animation company–the one of *Kill Bill* fame.

He worked hard–Japanese hard–from 7:30am to 10:00pm, including train rides. Still, in the late evenings after he came home he practiced at the piano. Not because he was told to, but because he wanted to.

Sometimes he called me long distance, "Papa, I'm sorry. I only practiced two hours today." More often than not I had to tell him to take a break. He never had to be told to practice.

Benjamin decided to participate in a state-wide (they are called prefectures in Japan) piano competition in western Japan. He planned to do it just for the fun of it. Perhaps he would add the results of the competition to his resume, if they were satisfactory. The other contestants chose a Beethoven piece–*Moonlight Serenade*, or a Mozart concerto–something light-hearted that everyone would recognize, or a Chopin etude–even non-classical music enthusiasts could hum along or tap their feet. Benjamin, however, chose to perform an extremely difficult Bach Toccata–two melodies going on at the same time but played out of synch. He played it flawlessly.

Benjamin is not a genius. One of his teachers defined for me that a genius musician or even an exceptionally talented piano player could learn a new piece in a relatively short time, usually within four to six hours of continual effort. Benjamin must spend four to six hours each day for four to six days, or more, to keep up with those 'geniuses.' Calling someone talented is often an excuse for not making the sacrifices that are necessary to excel. Benjamin does not commit himself to a schedule; rather he commits himself to learning, no matter the sacrifices he must make. His 'talent' is to work hard. But then, a father would think that about his son, wouldn't he?

Benjamin won the prefecture-wide competition; took first place in the open division. His competitors came from all over Japan, including other young men and women who had graduated from music schools and so on. There were congratulatory remarks flying everywhere and his normal stern disciplined countenance turned briefly upside-down into a smile. Someone even thought to call his teacher, Kosugi-san, a renowned pianist throughout Japan, and congratulate Kosugi-san on a job well done by one of his pupils. Kosugi-san responded, "There is no need to congratulate me. Benjamin never listens to me. He always does as he pleases." The boy was just a boy. Perhaps he listened more than was thought, but in the end, he did what he thought was best.

Someone overheard one of the judges remark, "I would never play that piece in a competition."

> "Why?" another judge countered.
> "It's too difficult."
> "Yeah, and...?"
> "I would play something easier so I would have a better chance of winning. I can't believe that young man chose such a difficult piece."
> "You're right. But the boy still played it and in this place."
> "Benji, did you hear what those judges were saying about you?" his mother asked.
> "Un," was his reply, in Japanese. It is a one syllable version of the English equivalent "Uh-huh" and means the same thing.

Later in the evening, Benji telephoned me internationally to let me know about the competition. After recounting the above he concluded by telling me, "Papa, I didn't know I wasn't supposed to be able to play such a difficult piece in a competition. I thought I should play something I like, something I could put all of my effort into."

> "Yep, Benjamin, you should do what *you* want," I said.
> Benjamin responded, "Papa, I guess I was a bumblebee that day."

The motivator? For lack of a better word - blind ignorance.

I don't mean ignorance as in stupidity. Rather as in unknowing. And blind as in not looking as opposed to unable to physically see.

If you don't know that you can't do something you can much more likely achieve a goal. Too often we hear the voices of the naysayers. I cannot hear them. Nor does my son, Benjamin, listen.

If you think you can or you think you can't you are right.

The little train that could ... "I think I can, I think I can ..."

When it comes to blogging, know you can. With this little book and the knowledge it contains you can acheive your blogging goals.

The hardest part is getting from where you are to your keyboard. Then staying faithful.

Blogging is easy. Just hit the keyboard enough times. It's getting and staying motivated that is hard.

I think I have the solution to this most difficult problem. Please consider joining www .billbelew.com/subscribe. It is here where I pour out my heart and soul and make myself accessible to keep all the members on track.

I really really want you to succeed. I love blogging and what it has done for me. I know what it can do for you. Let me help.

Thanks for reading. See you in the blogosphere as we all work to:

Make a difference!

Bill

FAQ

FAQ 1. Why should someone want to blog?

There are at least two kinds of writers: those who write for writing's sake and those who write to be read. I am the second kind.

Further, there are at least two kinds of writers who write to be read" those who do it for the fun of it and those who would like to make some money doing the writing thing. This would include those who have written a book or two and want to get the word out. Again, I am the second kind.

Reason 1. Blogging pays my mortgage. I earn enough from my blogs to pay my sizable Silicon Valley mortgage. And I have had a book of my blog material published to boot. See *Gee I Wish I Had Been Drinking at the Time*. A second book is ***How Wilby Got 20 Million People to Read His Blogs and How You Can, Too***.

It is estimated that there are more than 77 million blogs. The general wisdom is that if there are that many, some of them have to be good. Why shouldn't mine be one of the good ones? Why shouldn't yours?

Blog is a contraction for the term *web log*. Frankly, the name is not very attractive. It sounds too much like blah, blah, blahg. I prefer to explain what I do: I keep content current and focused on one topic on an interactive website, in a log format presented in reverse chronological order.

Too often, those who don't know what blogs can be think bloggers just blah, blah, blahg about themselves—what they ate, the breakup in their relationship, or the kind of video games they like. Some bloggers do write like this. They are the ones who blahg, that is, they write for writing's sake.

Not all bloggers just blahg, though.

Some make it a serious effort. For example, four of the top eight online entertainment sites are blogs. More people read blogs than read *People, TV Guide, Entertainment Weekly,* or AskMen.com online. Often, a blogger can pass on information faster than major media sources. I wrote a couple of posts about the $700 billion man, Neel Kashkari, as breaking news, and more than 5,000 people read it.

Reason 2. It's fun to get an immediate response to what I write and from people who don't know me. I should also admit that I don't always, even usually, like the feedback I get.

Blogging is a global phenomenon. I own a blog network. You can discover it starting at PanAsianBiz.

Reason 3. I have writers who blog for me who live in India, Romania, Malaysia, Bangladesh, and America. Having such a global reach is a thrill. Did I mention that that blogging can be fun?

Reason 4. Blogging can be profitable. For bloggers the average annual revenue is $6,000. Those who can get 100,000 unique visitors a month, however, earn closer to $75,000. That income can be generated with minimum investment and a lot of hard work. There's the rub. Blogging is easy work if all you want to do is see your work on the net. Blogging is hard work if you want to make a living at it.

Reason 5: Blogging can be an effective way of getting publicity for your book, too. In the course of blogging I have gained more than 6,000 subscribers, that is, readers who want to see all the updates of my blogs.

The publisher of my book *Gee I Wish I Had Been Drinking at the Time* was quite happy to learn that I already had an audience of potential readers as well as visitors in the thousands who came to my sites.

FAQ 2. What does it mean to be a professional blogger?

I consider myself to be a professional blogger. By that I mean I pay my sizable Silicon Valley mortgage through income earned from blogging.

The resourceful reader can easily look up my address and go to Zillow or some other such site to find out how much I owe on my house and subsequently how much money that means.

Blogging income is the primary source of income for my family of three: wife, Mia Mei, and me. This means I earn *more* than my mortgage.

Blogging *for money.* This does not mean earning money is my primary purpose in life. Good golly no. Nor does it mean that blogging for money is the only reason I blog. It means that in future posts, I will tell readers how to blog if they want to make money at it.

Here is my Introduction to Blogging or 5 Reasons Why I Blog.

Will Rogers said, "If you can do it, it ain't bragging."

I have done it, and I will share with readers how I make money blogging.

FAQ 3. How many kinds of bloggers are there?

There are two kinds of bloggers. There are those who make money at blogging and those who do not. There are those who would blog whether anybody read their stuff or not, and there are those who want people to read what they wrote—and perhaps make some money or even a lot of money while that happens.

Make no mistake, I am the second kind. I want people to read my blogs and I want to make some money at it.

BLOGGING FOR MONEY – TIP 1

Make up your mind about which kind of blogger you are.

If you are just in this for the fun of it, then you are in the wrong place. You can leave now and my feelings will not be hurt. I wasn't writing to you anyway.

If you want to make money at blogging consider subscribing to this blog by putting your email in the box at the top in the middle column and I will tell you how I do it.

FAQ 4. Should a blogger be part of a network of other bloggers?

A newbie blogger for money might wonder, "Should I go it alone?" or "Should I join a network?"

"Should I go it alone?" = Is all I need to do is sit down and write?

"Should I join a network?" = Is it important to be part of a network of other bloggers?

Repeat after me: "Join a network of other bloggers. Be part of a network of other bloggers. Do not try to go it alone."

I have written about this at:

5 reasons to write for a blog network instead of going it alone.

and

The Power of a Blog Network – Part 1 of 2

and

The Power of a Blog Network – Part 2 of 2

I started blogging at a time when I was, to be frank, tired of being in the classroom. I had been teaching (still do but online now) in a classroom for 25 years (yeah, old people can do the blogging thing, too). More precisely, I was tired of the drama of dealing with people day in and day out.

I thought blogging would be an isolated venture. I was wrong. I learned rather quickly how important it was to be part of a network.

FAQ 5. How do bloggers decide on the domain name for their blogs?

Wilby blogging for money

I give workshops on blogging. I get asked to speak a lot on the topic. I even host Meetups on the topic. People come. They come by the 20s, 30s. and 40s (not their ages! The number of people).

I sell my <u>services</u>. Somehow that doesn't sound good coming from a preacher. My consulting services, I should say.

I also offer to be taken to breakfast or lunch for a free consultation. They pay and I answer questions. My sizable waistline will attest to how often I have been taken up on this.

Believe it or not, the two greatest challenges for beginning bloggers for money are what to write about and what to call their blog.

Seriously, people ask me all the time, "What should I call my blog?" and "What should I write about?"

How the dickens should I know what other people want to write about or call themselves?

I also offer to exchange emails for free (I might need to rethink this because of the abuse of my time). But I often have to cut people off because they cannot choose a name.

Toyota is taken. Apple is taken. The really good names are already taken.

I have some really stupid names for some of my most trafficked blogs: <u>PanAsianBiz</u>, <u>Filmyfair</u>, <u>RisingSunOfNihon</u>. Stupid names and yet they still have gone over several million views.

The point: the name doesn't matter all that much. Really.

Here are my three suggestions:

---

1. Pick something that is easy to remember.
2. Make sure the name is easy to speel, spiel, speirl, I mean spell.
3. When all else fails, use your name. Unless, of course, nobody knows how to spell it.

But for goodness sake, pick a name.

FAQ 6. What happens if you don't like the name after you decide on it?

My son started his blog at the domain <u>MephistoApe</u>.

He didn't get a lot of traffic, but over time some people, at least those who could spell, got used to the name or had it bookmarked. Somehow they could find it.

Well, over time his musical career began to take off. And sponsors, venues, and others began to ask him if he had a website.

Benjamin Belew, Creator of Wilby

It sounded dumb to tell professional venues that he had a name they couldn't understand. So, he wanted to change the name, BUT he didn't want to lose what he had already started. So what to do?

He went to (actually I went to) GoDaddy and bought the domain name <u>BenjaminBelew. Those who typed in </u>www.mephistoape.comwere redirected to the new BenjaminBelew site. Even the technically challenged like myself could do that. And when all else fails there's a phone number to call for GoDaddy and little boys and girls answer and talk with you until your problems are solved. Really!

Now my son can tell friends and/or potential venues that he can be found at MephistoApe or at BenjaminBelew. Either will take readers to the same site.

Say you have a pretty well-trafficked blog and have thought of a better name AND that name is available? Buy the new domain name and direct it to the old blog. Problem solved.

FAQ 7. How important is the tagline for your blog?

Creating a tagline is like coming up with a thesis for an essay, only shorter.

A tagline is the heart and soul of what a blog is about—in ten words or less—no prepositions, and no articles if you can get away with it.

The tagline is one of the first items a search engine will come across. The tagline tells the search engines what your blog is about. It also tells the reader what your blog is about.

My tagline for this blog appears right under my name. Look up the page, right under Bill Belew.

Business of Blogging for Money

That's a mouthful. Good keywords and lots of possible keyword combinations.

A tagline is also a valuable device for the bloggers that will remind them at all times what they are writing about.

Little league has nothing to do with the business of blogging for money. If I get off topic I'll know it.

To read much more about taglines check out this post by Anti: Tagline – The 10 Words That Make or Break Your Blog.

What's your blog about? In 10, count 'em, words or less.

FAQ 8. How many categories should a blog have?

You can always tell when a blogger has been around for a while. The blogger's category list becomes the determining factor for how long the front page is.

I know because I have been there, done that. I started thinking everything was going to be a new category in my blog... Not! I had 50 to 60 categories on more than one blog.

My take: a blog should not have more than 10 to 12 categories.

For example, my blog PanAsianBiz (PAB) is divided up into Asia News, World News, Entertainments, Sports, Jobs, Exams, Technology, Business, Featured and Weird. These are the parent categories. Under Asia news, there are countries. Under entertainment are different kinds of entertainment. Under sports, various sports. And so on.

Before giving a topic of a post category status, ask yourself, "Can I say at least 100 more things about this?" If not, put it under a parent category. If you have more than 10 to 12 categories that you can say 100 or more things about, create a new blog altogether.

I started back in 2006 writing about Asia, but had so much to say about Japan and China that PAB spawned ZhonghuaRising and RisingSunOfNihon.

Ten to twelve categories. No more.

FAQ 9. What is the best blogging software?

Considering that I am writing this with WordPress, the obvious answer is, well, lemme think about it for a moment. Um... WordPress.

More adventures of Wilby

I started blogging on freebie site writingup.com. It is now defunct, their servers are gone, as is everything I wrote with it. So, I know that's not a good option.

I then worked with a new start-up blog network that used Typepad. They started to make the transition to WordPress but, before it was complete, they also went belly up.

I then experimented with Blogger for a while but got spammed to death.

I now am writing for a large online media company that has its own software. And it freezes up ALL the time so that's no good.

Don't knock it until you try it, they said. So I tried them.

All of my blogs on WordPress greet me every time I log in. Like a faithful dog, it is always there—when I am in a bad mood, good mood, or otherwise. WordPress has never let me down.

One time I couldn't figure out how to do something on WordPress. It didn't interfere with my being able to post; it had more to do with being found and indexing and that kind of thing. It happened to me about the time of a WordCamp in San Francisco—HQ to WP. I went to the WordCamp, walked up to the genius bar, and the nerdy little tweep behind the bar had the problem solved in less time than it took me to write this post.

Repeat after me: WordPress. WordPress.

If you are not blogging on WordPress, sooner or later you will. So, you might as well start out on it or go ahead and make the switch later.

FAQ 10. What is the best template to use?

Choosing the right and the best template is the topic of tip 8 in the Blogging for Money series.

There is no right template. There certainly is no best template.

More adventures of Wilby

If it's not the name of the blog that causes would-be bloggers to stop dead in their tracks, or the tagline, picking a template will do it every time.

I remember when I first went to Japan. It was some five years before I returned to the States. My first trip to the supermarket for something I recognized caused me to stop dead. I could not believe how many kinds of bread there were, how many different types of cereal there were, how many...how many. Suddenly I couldn't choose.

In the car on the way home I tried to find a familiar radio station. It was gone but there were other stations every 10 hertz along the dial. I couldn't decide on one.

Cable TV—same problem. I kept thinking there might be something on another channel that I wanted to watch more. By the time I got through all the channels I couldn't remember what it was I wanted to watch. And when I could remember what it was I couldn't remember which channel it was. And when I did finally find the program, invariably it was already over.

The point: **pick a template and make it work for you**. Choose your favorite color. And flip a coin for two columns or three. Then go with it. It can always be changed later.

The template this blog is on is free. Mia Mei's Morsels (my two-year-old) is a free template and I think it's kind of neat. I once spent $75 to get exactly the template I wanted, and I bought the right to use it at more than one site. I don't use it anymore.

Pick a WordPress template, any WordPress template, and make it work.

FAQ 11. What's the best way to monitor the performance of your blog?

When blogging for money, I found that the one non-WordPress item I could NOT get along without was the sitemeter.

I used to do triathlons. I can't imagine swimming laps without counting how many I had done. Or riding a bike without knowing how fast or how far I had gone. And invariably, whenever I ran somewhere, the first chance I got I took my bike to measure the distance. Before long, I knew exactly how far it was between any two possible points I might take between my house and work.

The point is **a sitemeter will tell you how well you are doing**.

The free version is more than adequate, even if it only goes back to the previous 100. I have the paid version at two of my sites but only because somebody gave it to me. I never go anywhere on the paid version that I can't go on the free version.

What about Google Analytics?

Truth is, I have Google Analytics installed at all my sites. But, I never go there. Reason? There is too much information.

I know a LOT of bloggers who get lost watching their advanced versions of sitemeter or their Google Analytics or their Quantcast reports or their Omniture Reports. And all the while that they are analyzing, they are not writing.

There is nothing that any of those services can provide that a blogger can't learn from the free version of sitemeter. But just for the fun of it, I'd also install Google Analytics.

Instructions on how to install Sitemeter on your site can be found at Sitemeter.

FAQ 12. Should you use free or paid hosting?

A lot of bloggers get their feet wet on the free WordPress version.

You can't make money on the free WordPress version. Nor should you be able to. Why should the likes of WordPress provide anyone a place to earn money for free? Would you?

You can start out on the free version until you get traffic and then make the switch to paid hosting. This is for the really cheap, um, frugal person. Indeed, it does make sense.

When it comes to paid hosting, no one service is any better than any other.

I started out with GoDaddy and many of my smaller sites still remain there. My larger sites are on dedicated servers.

I like GoDaddy (they pay me nothing to say this) because when I have trouble a little girl or boy will actually answer the phone and talk with me until I get my problem resolved.

If you can find a better service, go with them. But don't agonize and don't shop around till you can't decide. Pick one and make it work.

Another advantage to paid hosting is that you have more flexibility with your templates...as in, you can't see particulars in the sitemeter on a free WordPress blog, but you can if it is on a paid server.

The best and cheapest place to get a domain and hosting is BM2Hosting.com.

Consider the old axiom: you have to spend money to make money. Spring for your own domain name and paid hosting, which is about $10 per month in the beginning.

FAQ 13. When do you place advertisements on your blog?

Simple math is involved. Or if you really dislike numbers, just jump to the bottom and I'll tell you.

Suppose you can earn $2 for every 1,000 pages viewed at your site from the likes of Google AdSense. This is, by the way, how ad rates are discussed. Earnings per 1,000 or ecpm.

Google only pays when you get total earnings of $50. This means you need to have 25,000 visits/views before you can make $50.

If your site is getting 100 views a day (check your sitemeter), you are earning $2 every 10 days (or $6/month or $50 every 9 months).

Do NOT put ads on your site when you are getting just 100 views a day because they just clutter up the look. 200 views a day is too soon. 300, 400, 500? Maybe.

At 500 views a day the blogger can earn $2/2 days or $30/month-ish. That's gas money, and you can collect almost every month.

My recommendation is that when you start regularly seeing 500 views a day, you can start putting ads up. But don't go crazy with them.

FAQ 14. Do bloggers get exposure in their industry?

There is more than one way to make money from blogging. But blogging is the common thread.

Plus alpha is a term I picked up when I was in Japan. It means that something is at heart, but there is an intangible that sometimes comes along—a plus that starts with *alpha* as in the Greek alphabet. No, there is no plus beta. At least I have never heard the term.

Probloggers: "71% have a greater visibility in their industry," says a survey I read.

A friend of mine has a blog <u>TheWeeklyDriver</u>. I contributed to his site for about six months. During that time, a new car showed up at my front door every week. A Jaguar (no kidding!), a Land Rover, and so on. I wrote a review and a new car showed up with a tank of gas and free insurance.

And all I had to do was write a review of what I thought of the experience.

Why am I NOT still doing this? Remember the GM, Ford car crisis and crunch? I was one of the last to be asked to do the reviews and one of the first to be let go. It was a great gig while it lasted. And somebody had to do it.

The point: Because I had a blog and visibility, I was asked to drive. And that counts as money in my book. According to one car company, chances are good that I will be driving again come this January.

FAQ 15. Can bloggers sell products from their sites?

This is the second in a short series of four posts from a larger series of a yet-to-be-determined number of posts in the Blogging for Money series.

Money can be earned from blogging and it is NOT always about traffic. Though a good visible blog opens doors to other avenues. See plus alpha 1 of 4.

Survey says, "63% (of probloggers) say, 'Clients have purchased their products and services.'"

This means two out of three bloggers who reach a certain level find that they acquire clients who in turn purchase products and services they offer.

I have a book. People buy it. It's up in the right-hand corner of this site. However, if people don't read this post or some other post, they're not likely to know about the book, right?

So I offer consulting services. They get tapped into—a lot!

And I don't just get paid to talk about blogging! I'll explain that in the next post.

The point is that blogging opens doors to other avenues of income as well.

FAQ 16. Do bloggers get any respect?

This is the third of four in a spin-off of a longer series about blogging for money.

More exposure.

Survey also says, "56% say, 'they are now regarded as a thought leader.'"

I am a Christian and I am not ashamed to admit it. I maintain the Christian Worldview Examiner. Earlier this year I was asked to speak at a national Christian convention on blogging and getting the Word out. The *Word* being God's Word, of course.

Even earlier this year, I was asked to be a part-time and interim pastor for a new startup church. That church eventually hired me to be a full-time and permanent pastor. (I have enough work now to be full time three times over, which I'll explain in future posts.)

Anyway, the tipping point in being hired by the church was shared with me by one of the members of the hiring committee.

"We read your Christian site and we liked what you said there. That's why we hired you."

A thought leader. Yes.

A leader who thinks. Yes.

Blogging got me into another job I love to do. And I don't have to give up blogging to do it!

FAQ 17. Do bloggers get asked to speak at conferences about their specialty?

There is money to be made from blogging in ways other than just pecking.

Visibility.

Selling products and services.

Being a thought leader.

The last: A survey of probloggers, "40% say, 'they have been asked to speak at conferences.'"

I spoke twice last week to two group: one of 46 people and one of 36 people. They gave me around $600 (real number) for the two appearances.

Here is a partial list of speaking engagements I did this year. However I fail to keep it updated because it's too much trouble and because it changes all the time.

The point is being a problogger allows me to speak on the topic.

Being a problogger about a topic will allow you to become a speaker on the circuit about that topic. For sure. How do I know? Because I get asked to speak at Christian conventions and the like. See plus alpha 3 of 4.

There's more than one way to make money from blogging.

FAQ 18. How does a blogger decide what to write about?

Some might wonder why this would even come up. But, to be sure, I get asked a LOT, "What should I write about?"

This is as if to say, "Tell me what are the best topics to write about so I can get the most traffic and make the most money."

The old adage "write what you know" is true in the blogosphere as well.

As much writing as needs to be done to make a living at this (I will address this in a future post), it would be quite miserable an experience to always have to write about something you have no or just a cursory interest in.

When I started out, I pitched the idea to a business blog network of writing about business in Asia, a topic I not only knew something about, but also had an interest in. Having started a business in Asia and using my second language, I felt I had something to share as well.

Business in Asia was not a hot burning topic, however, nor was it expected to bring in a lot of traffic. That was well over 20 million page views ago.

There are something like 100,000 left-handed quilters in the U.S. alone. I don't know how many are online, but if you can find a niche and become the expert or the go-to place, your site has the potential to attract readers and earn money.

I spend a lot of time sitting with people and trying to help them narrow down their topic. I guess that's why students have trouble coming up with a thesis statement for their essays.

Write what you know in such a way that other people who are interested in your topic will come to see what you have to say about it. And those who weren't interested in the topic will find out why you are.

FAQ 19. What trumps passion when choosing what to blog about?

Believe it or not there is something that trumps passion when it comes to choosing a topic to blog about. This is the point of tip 17.

Write what you know.

Write what you are passionate about.

Write about a topic that has good potential appeal to advertisers.

Write about something that has a potential for a lot of content.

Those are good tips, but I can think of something else that trumps them all when it comes to being motivated to write.

Drum roll, please ...

Hunger.

A guy and, more importantly, his family have to eat.

If I could have chosen anything for my first blog topic, it would not have been Pan Asian Business. But I was offered the job, and I knew some things about the topic. Most of all I knew I wasn't going to let my family go hungry.

The short answer is when you are choosing a topic, choose one:

---

1. You know something about.
2. You have an interest in (the stronger the better).
3. That has a lot of potential content.
4. That has appeal to advertisers.
5. That you can write and write and write about until the traffic comes and the money follows.

Choose a topic when you are hungry and make that topic work.

FAQ 20. Can bloggers really find themselves in the spotlight?

Bloggers must ask themselves if they really enjoy being the center of attention.

Do they like being in the public spotlight?

Are they thick-skinned?

Invariably when I ask these questions at a blog workshop, I get a resounding response: "Yes!"

To which I reply, "That's not true."

"You like to be the center of attention and enjoy being in the public spotlight *when everyone around you agrees with you*."

It's a mystery to some degree. No matter how good the news is you have to share, there will almost always be someone there to tell you how not so good it is. Out of ten comments, nine might say you did well, but the tenth will let you know in no uncertain terms that you did not. Guess which response you will remember when you go to bed at night?

These days I find that it is mostly the contrarians from whom you will hear. Nine out of ten comments are negative and the tenth is positive. Maybe it's just me. Or maybe it's just my topics. If you have had a different experience, let me know.

Writers say they like feedback. That's not true: Writers like *positive* feedback. Negative feedback and the hair on their neck bristles. They get defensive.

Bloggers are no different.

If you want to make money blogging, you have to get traffic. And when the traffic comes and all eyes are on you, be ready to take the heat or, yeah, get out of the kitchen, um, blogosphere.

FAQ 21. Do bloggers need to be disciplined?

I seem to have begun addressing the characteristics of the blogger who is trying to make money in the past few posts. Looking at my notes, I have more to say in future posts as well. Tip 19 addresses self-discipline.

I am in my fifth year of trying to make a living at this blogging thing. I have more than 15,000 posts at my sites. That averages out to eight to ten posts per day since I started blogging.

I can honestly say that I have NEVER had anyone say to me, "Bill, you'd better go write on your blog now." Never, ever.

If you don't have self-discipline, if you are not a self-starter, you will not make money blogging. Plain and simple. Unless that is, you have deep pockets and you want to pay someone to do it for you.

Foodie mummy articulates her own struggle with this in her post Serious lack of self-discipline.

Even when you think of something to say you have to take the initiative to get that infrastructure in place.

Ask yourself, "Am I a self-starter? Do I have the discipline to stay with this?"

Be honest and listen to your answer. If it's no, then find something else to do. Blogging for money won't work for you.

FAQ 22. What is the time commitment a blogger needs to make?

Here is a simple law of the universe, articulated in different ways.

What you sow, you reap. You get what you pay for. Garbage in, garbage out.

Blogging tip 20 applies that law to making money with your blog. The more time you commit the more likely you are to see a return for your effort.

The blogger must be willing to make the time commitment.

Two men were sitting on the roof of the house of one of the men because their neighborhood was flooded. The water leveled off at about 6 feet.

One man pointed out to the other, "Look at the hat in Harry's front yard. It is going back and forth in a straight line."

"Yeah. Harry said that today come hell or high water he was going to mow his lawn."

The serious blogger wanting to make money at this (is that statement redundant?) must make the time commitment and honor that commitment.

As a benchmark—in my first 18 months of blogging I spent a minimum of 3 hours every day writing at least 15 posts a day.

Are you willing to make the time commitment?

FAQ 23. How important is a sense of humor?

Sooner or later if you are blogging for money, you are going to need a sense of humor. That's the point of tip 21.

Bloggers simply cannot take themselves too seriously.

ABCs of Evolution

Mistakes are made and there are a LOT of folk waiting to point that out to you when it happens.

Readers will assume you can't spell before they will think you just made a typo.

If you get a fact wrong, they will blame your mother.

If they don't agree with my opinion, they will call in the troops to attack.

I wrote a post The *ABCs of Evolution.*

I am a Christian and am not embarrassed by it. I think there is more than ample scientific evidence that God created the world in six 24-hourish days some 6,000 years ago. When I wrote that post, the atheists came a yelling at me.

They hated my post and me so much they called their friends, linked to the article at "we hate fundies" sites and they came a yelling at me.

Each time a comment is left on a post, it gives that particular post more "juice," more findability. (I will explain that in a future post.)

Now, if you search ABCs of Evolution you will find it is number one on Google and also front page on Bing and Yahoo.

Every time the haters came after me and left a comment, I thought to myself "ka-ching!"

That's the sound of money coming in.

Who has a sense of humor now?

FAQ 24. Which is more important, having an ego or humility?

It is pretty easy for some and I suppose I am not immune to thinking more of myself than I should when 60,000 people show up to my site in one day or for just one post!

The higher the number the bigger the ego. Blogging tip 22 encourages the blogger to balance his or her ego with some humility if the blogger wants to make money.

It is really, really easy and this I do not suppose, I know, to evaluate your self-worth by the number of visits or page views you are getting.

Numbers are up—feeling pretty good about myself.

Numbers are down—my little girl runs behind the sofa (not really!).

I have learned the answer to the question of what the next hot topic on the web will be.

Answer: nobody knows.

When I get good traffic, I no longer dislocate my arm by patting myself on the back. I become grateful and offer a prayer of thanks.

When I get bad traffic, I knuckle down and try harder.

It is hard to maintain an ego when you are in the service business and that's what a blogger is. Bloggers serve up content.

FAQ 25. How important is it that the blogger continues to learn?

if you want to make money blogging you need to have a pretty deep well of content. And, if you are anything like me, that means you have to keep replenishing yourself; learning on the grow.

After 15,000 posts I often get asked, "Don't you run out of things to write about?"

"Nope, not yet." And I don't reckon I ever will.

Not as long as the world turns and there are newsfeeds and books being written and bloggers blogging and ... and ...

When I was writing daily about news events in Asia, I opened up four or five Chinese newspapers, four or five Japanese newspapers, Korean newspapers, and so on.

I'd read through the headlines and open up tabs on topics I felt I had something to contribute. In about 20 minutes or so, I'd have twenty to thirty tabs opened up. Then Firefox would crash and I'd have to do it again.

With thirty ideas for topics, it was and is easy to come up with fifteen blog posts. And in the meantime, I was able to keep my pulse on a region of the world where I had lived for 20 years.

In a word, I was learning. I was keeping the content well primed.

If you want to blog for money, continue to learn.

FAQ 26. How important is social networking to the blogger?

Social networking is my weakest link. But Blogging for Money tip 24 drives home the need to be social, even virtually. And I am NOT talking about Facebook, LinkedIn, and the like. I will address those in future posts.

A blogger has to have friends, friends who write blogs, friends who read blogs, friends they link to and get backlinks from.

Dave at MyChinaConnection knows this well and has applied the principles well. I have been working with Dave from the get-go on his blog. He is one of the few who does what I told him to do.

He faithfully reads other blogs and links to them when appropriate. He gets in forums and on chats to make friends. And make friends he does. They, in turn, without his prompting post links to his site here and there. Those kinds of connections are golden, and the more a blogger has of them the better.

The results are in. Check out Dave's sitemeter and what he has been able to accomplish in just a few months.

If you want to grow your traffic = make more money: Make friends, real friends online.

And remember, you are NOT trying to make money off your friends. The money will come elsewhere.

FAQ 27. How important is creativity to the blogger?

I did a workshop last weekend in Carmel, CA (you know, home to Clint Eastwood? He wasn't there, btw.) The attendees were a group of writers from California Writers Club Central Coast.

I made what might be interpreted as a bold statement.

"I think everything has to do with everything. If you can't relate your topic to another topic, you are a lousy writer."

I am sure I have stretched this idea too far and even broken it from time to time, but I do think most every topic has to do with most every other topic.

That "being creative" connection opens up the door for bloggers to write about almost any topic in the world and what it has to do with their own topic of choice.

Pets? Coffee? Child rearing? Pick a topic, any topic, and I can tell you how it might manifest itself in Asia, for example. Or why it would NOT manifest itself there. That's a connection I can make.

If you can connect your topic to current events, for example, the world becomes your stage. And when all the world is your potential readership...well, by now you get the picture.

Be creative with your blog and the potential for more readers becomes much bigger.

FAQ 28. What's the number-one reason blogs fail?

The number-one reason why businesses and blogs fail is the subject of tip 26 in the Blogging for Money series.

The number-one reason businesses fail is that they (owners, workerbees) don't stay with their idea long enough for it to catch on.

The reasons can be/seem legitimate: running out of funds, broken relationships, and more.

But the bottom line (businesses use that word) is that the people who wanted their business to succeed just didn't stay with the idea long enough.

A blogger might run out of content, get distracted with "life," or some other reason. But it's the same.

The Japanese have a saying: '石の上にもう三年.' *Ishi no ue ni mo sannen.* It is pronounced *eeshee no uway knee moh sahn nen.* It means "sit on a rock for three years."

The Japanese use this saying when talking about starting a venture, particularly a business. The thought is, if a business can survive for three years, it will succeed.

If a blogger will stay with the blog for three years, writing faithfully and with good content (more on that in future posts, too), the blog will succeed.

If your blog is a good idea to start with, it is in all likelihood a good idea to see through until it catches on.

Stay with it.

FAQ 29. How important is it for the blogger to have a voice?

I knew a preacher who was very fond of saying, "If you aren't you, who's going to be you?"

Bob and Larry are fond of saying, "God made you special and he loves you very much."

Finding your voice is tip 27 in the Blogging for Money series.

What's this have to do with making money?

The blogosphere is cluttered with imitations, knockoffs, robobloggers, and automatic blog post generators.

I do not like using clichés, but indeed the cream does rise to the top. If you are you and your stuff is original, it will stand out. It will be found over time. It will get read = traffic comes. And traffic will translate to earnings.

I hired a writer from overseas a long time ago and he copied and pasted too much. He eventually came around, and now people copy and paste from him.

He really gets it now.

Be you. Then watch out for cheap imitations.

FAQ 30. What is the standard for hard work?

Nobody told me how hard it would be to make money at blogging. I will share with you a few of the standards I set for myself, which in the end paid off, in tip 28.

I have met a few bloggers who said, "I have blogged a LOT this week."

"How much?"

"I wrote three posts this week."

Three posts is NOT a lot.

Technorati considers a blog that gets updated once a month to be an active blog.

I do not consider that active.

As I write this, it happens to be the time for NaNoWriMo. Writers all over the world are committed to writing a novel—good, bad, and ugly—in one month. The goal is 50,000 words in the month of November. Get it down on paper first, and then revise it. You can't revise what you don't have...that sort of thing.

50,000 words in a month?!

When I kicked off my blogs, I wrote at least 15 posts each day with a minimum of 200 words per post. And I did that 30 days a month.

Let's do the math: 15 x 200 = 3,000 words daily x 30 days = 90,000 words.

I did that monthly for the first 18 months of my blogs.

There may be blogs that put out more content in a month using a team of writers, but I don't know which blog it is.

There might be more prolific bloggers than me, but I don't know them either.

That was the standard I set for myself. And it worked for me.

How long did it take me to do that much work each day? I'll answer that tomorrow.

Nobody said it was going to be easy.

FAQ 31. How long does it take to write a post?

Quick recap. I wrote 15 posts a day x 200 words/post for 30 days/month.

I did this while teaching full time at the college level both at a physical location and online.

I worked on my kitchen table while my mother-in-law cooked greasy Chinese food and my father-in-law watched sports program after sports program in our little two-bedroom, one-bath condominium in Campbell. The extra bedroom was my office, but they slept there and at the time I had never heard of Panera Bread. (I am sitting in a Panera Bread shop as I write this.)

I can write fifteen 200-word blog posts, including doing the research and inserting images, and providing credits and links to any sources I used in about 3 hours, sometimes 4 (but not usually more than that). I didn't have the time!

Depending on the objective of your post, it shouldn't take you longer than 15 to 20 minutes to type it, illustrate it, link it, and publish it.

Keep in mind that this is a "regular" post, not an "evergreen" post. I will explain the difference in a future tip.

Now stop thinking and write.

FAQ 32. Do bloggers need to take a break?

Having addressed working hard in the past two tips on blogging for money, it seemed fitting to me to address when to take a break.

Indeed I may not be the right person to address that.

On my plate at the moment is writing a sermon (I am the full-time pastor for a startup church in Silicon Valley), reading the final draft of a dissertation (I am a dissertation mentor), providing feedback to a new professor (I mentor new professors for an online university), and packing my bags to meet a friend to drive to Sacramento to participate in a 50K fund-raising run. This morning I had a breakfast meeting and I am writing this while waiting for a lunch meeting.

My good friend, when he has days that are especially productive, calls them "Bill Belew days". I CAN get a lot done. It does not always mean I do things well as I might like. I do, however, always give it my best.

But ...

I have also been on extended cruises to the Caribbean and to Alaska. My son was a national class swimmer in college and had meets throughout the country. I attended all of them. And never missed a beat in my blogging.

Repeat after me: "Thank God for the scheduler."

Indeed the days leading up to such events were a bit harder, but I still got things done and I enjoyed being on the pool side or watching glaciers crash.

Learn how to use the scheduler and take a break from time to time.

Come to think of it. I need a break now.

FAQ 33. How important is it for the blogger's content to be original?

My first best tip for search engine optimization (SEO) is to write original content.

Nothing beats original content. Nothing.

The web is filled with redundancy. There are automated bloggers that will take your stuff and translate it into other languages, then translate it back into English in hopes of making it more findable.

Whatever you write and publish will be time stamped and be yours if it is indeed yours, that is original-to-you content. Stuff that comes out of your head and not somebody else's head is yours. Everything else is not.

In the academic world there is quoting, paraphrasing, summarizing, and plagiarizing and original content as a result of research and experience. To be sure they all happen in the blogosphere as well.

All of them are acceptable in your blog posts except the last.

Start with original content, summarize, when need be, paraphrase if it is called for, quote others (but not too much—twenty words or less) and NEVER steal.

Do this and your posts will go a long way.

FAQ 34. How long should a post be?

If you knew how stupid I have been you might stop reading here. SEO technique 2 in the Blogging for Money series is about post length.

For the first 2 years of my blogging life I thought posts had to be 200 words long or more. So I diligently wrote 200 words. Come what may, I made it 200 words each and every post.

Then I found out that a post only needed to be 100 words long to make it into a search engine.

Remember, this is about blogging for money. It's different than blogging for other reasons. The astute reader will notice that in this series of tips I am always over 100 words. This is because I am NOT blogging for money here, I am trying to teach something. It's different.

When blogging for money, 100 words is all you need. Original words.

How do I know that?

I have two ways of knowing.

People in the know told me at the beginning of my blogging career that a post needed to be 100 words. I totally missed the instruction and didn't rediscover it until 2 years AFTER a ton of posts that were 200 words in length.

Come to think of it, I could have had twice as many posts in my archives.

The other way I know it is that some of my blogs get published in Google News. Every now and then a post will not get accepted and I get feedback on why. The number-one reason? The post is too short. I play around with length until I know what works and what doesn't. One hundred words-ish was the limit. Any idea how much people would pay to know this tidbit, or how much time I spent learning it?

I'd write 125 words and call it a post.

But what do you do if what you have to say takes more than 100 words?

FAQ 35. What should I do when I am getting long-winded?

What happens when you have more to say than 100 words will let you?

My post yesterday had 315 words and I still had more to say.

I decided to finish the thought in this post.

That's the answer.

If you have more to say than a post will allow, divide it into two or three or more posts and call it part 1, part 2, etc.

Use the same title (if it's good) and add a number or some sort of way to make it known it's a continuation of something else you were writing.

Link back to the other post and, in the former post, link to the continuation of your writing.

In this way, readers will hopefully click-through increasing your overall traffic.

And that IS what you want, isn't it?

For your readers to spend more time on your site?

FAQ 36. Should bloggers include images in their posts?

On almost any given day about 10% of the traffic to my sites come to find an image that I have included in one of my posts. That is SEO technique 4 in the Blogging for Money series.

I didn't do that at the beginning, but I almost NEVER fail to include some sort of image when I am writing a post.

I used the Wilby images in this series just because I wanted to. I want to call attention to my son, Benjamin Belew, the creator of Wilby, and the things he can do.

Of course, the images should not be stolen and every effort should be made to give credit where it's due, mentioning the name of the photographer if possible.

I almost always (unless I forget) provide a link to wherever I found the image, at another blogger's site or otherwise. The blogger is invariably happy to have the back link and I am happy to have the image.

I have posted more than 15,000 images over the years and I can still count on one hand the number of times I was yelled out for "stealing," which I didn't.

When that happens, I just take the image down and send an apology.

FAQ 37. Should captions be placed on images?

If you don't have an image, clip art or an animation-type image will work, too.

Most important than including an image is including a caption on the image so it becomes searchable.

A friend of mine once wrote a post about Michael Jordan's Air Jordan shoes. Yeah, remember those?

He STILL gets traffic for that post.

It is not enough to just stick something in your post to look at.

The image has to be something that is relevant to the topic of your post. And the best way to show that is to give the image a caption that is relevant to the topic of the post.

Yeah, I know...Wilby is not relevant to blogging. But if I write about the two of them in concert enough, in time he will be. At least that's my goal.

FAQ 38. Should a blogger link to others?

I want to point out the importance of including an external link to another site, another blogger's site.

When bloggers link to other bloggers it creates link love.

It shows the other bloggers that you think highly enough of their stuff to link to it.

If the other bloggers are worth their salt they will see the back link and come to your site to see who is saying what about them.

Then, if they feel so inclined, they will reciprocate.

It doesn't always happen; it doesn't usually happen anymore. But it does still happen.

Those links are gold to a blogger and search engine findability.

For example, SEOMoz ranks external links of second importance among the Top 5 Ranking Factors.

Indeed, I couldn't agree more. And I am also inclined to read on to learn what other good and practical stuff TL has to say.

FAQ 39. Should a blogger link to him- or herself?

Including internal links is SEO technique 7 in the Blogging for Money series.

In short, this is all about linking to other related posts within your blog to the topic in the post at hand.

This is easier than ever with a WordPress plug in. The plug in will scour your site to find other posts with similar words and content and provide links to other similar posts.

Linking to yourself is not as powerful as having someone else link to you, but it does give your site internal connectivity.

When readers come across something they like at one post, chances and hopes are they will click-through to other posts. Telling them where they can go (not where to go) is a service the interested readers appreciate.

Including internal links can keep readers at your site longer, giving more visibility to well-placed and relevant ads you might have at your site as well.

And that results in higher return for your effort.

FAQ 40. How important is it to choose good keywords?

An important point about content. Search engine robots are stupid. (That's the pot calling the kettle black, some might say). Search engines cannot read content. They look for character or letter combinations.

SEO looks like S E O and blog looks like b l o g. The search engine is not reading the word. It can't read. It can only see characters and letters and match the characters SEO in this blog with the same characters in another blog post.

Does this make sense?

This is why good use of keywords is important. However, there is a point (somewhere in the algorithms) where the search engine realizes this combination of characters and letters should not be appearing this often and this close together within this word count. How do they do that? When that happens, it is a kind of spam. Keyword spam.

The point—write naturally and use keywords when they work.

I have been guilty of forcing it, and it has gotten me nowhere.

Use keywords well, but use them naturally, too.

FAQ 41. How important are tags to a post?

Not long ago, members of the Google AdSense team came to speak at one of my Meetups. See the sidebar if you happen to live in the Silicon Valley area if you'd like to attend a meetup related to blogging, writing, SEO, WordPress, and the like.

Google's headquarters are just a few miles from my house, as are Yahoo's and Apple's. Which I suppose is neither here nor there.

The Google AdSense team alluded to the fact that tags are not even relevant to search engine results. But then they qualified that statement by saying they really don't know anything about the search engine side of things and their expertise is in AdSense. They did offer tips on ad placement. I will talk about that in a future post.

Nevertheless, for me, old habits are hard to break. WordPress has a box to the right of where I am writing this post that begs for posting tags. So, I will put words in there that appear in this post that are relevant to this article that I do not usually use.

And to be sure, I have seen when checking my referral pages that search engines have found me through a tag that I created for a post.

WARNING: Do not use more than three or four tags, maximum five, but NOT six. This is called tag spamming, and it does no good. Furthermore it looks stupid.

FAQ 42. What is blog authority?

Blog sites that have authority go farther than blog sites that do not.

Authority is measured by how many other sites link to you and how many sites link to them.

I am fond of saying that search engines are stupid. They don't know I have two terminal degrees. They don't know how long I spent in Asia, and how well I can speak Japanese, Chinese, and Russian.

Search engines don't know anything about me personally or professionally.

The search engines only know how many other sites (people) have come to my site and thought enough about my content to link to it = refer it to their readers. And how many of those sites that linked to me had people link to them.

I am also fond of saying to all my writer friends that it is easy to write. You (they) can even be the best writers in the whole wide world (my daughter told me to say that), but if nobody reads it, nobody knows.

It is easy to write. It is hard to get read.

People get read when others tell them to read you. *That* is authority.

How to build authority for your site....I'll talk about that in the next post.

FAQ 43. How does a blogger build authority?

I can think of twenty or more ways to build authority.

I will go through them one by one in future posts. But for now, I want to tell you a couple that I think are the most important.

The problem with the information age is that we are inundated with information. We now need someone to sort through all the information and tell us what is important and what is fluff.

I can remember teaching one of my college classes. I presented both sides of an argument so thoroughly, I suppose, that one student finally threw up his hands in exasperation and said, "Mr. Belew, just tell us what is right!"

Just because I know twenty or thirty ways to increase authority to your site, it doesn't mean they are all useful.

Two things are more important than all others.

The first is engage with other bloggers. Find other bloggers who write about the same thing you do and engage with them. Read their stuff, comment. Contact them and tell them they are good and do NOT ask for anything in return. Be genuine. And when it makes sense, link to their sites.

Nothing will beat that.

And remember, the reason bloggers want authority is because it will make their sites/posts more findable. Findability = traffic, and we know what more traffic means.

Oh, and as Darth Vader is famous for saying, "There is another."

FAQ 44. What kinds of content are good?

Anyone who has read any portion of the first forty tips will remember that I like to say that search engines are stupid. Search engines cannot make value judgments. They only check for character-letter combinations and numbers of links in and out.

The more consistent you are with your keyword usage = staying on topic, the more the search engines will respond.

The more people you link to and who link to you the better. Keep in mind that those who link to you will have other folks linking to them as well. Search engines will respond.

A search engine cannot say something has good or bad content. The search engine can only determine that a post has good structure—good keyword usage, images, links, and so on, but it cannot make the evaluation: "that's good writing."

In subsequent posts I'd like to define what I think good writing is.

And I define good writing as that which pleases the reader AND the search engines, preferably in that order.

The list now; the explanations to follow in future posts. Good writing:

1. Adds something unique.
2. Contains something people want to know about.
3. Makes a contribution to the discussion.
4. Has a great title.
5. Never runs out of ideas.
6. Is timely.
7. Can attract repeat traffic.
8. Engages the readers.
9. Has pillar content.
10. Can go viral.
11. Draws in subscribers.
12. Has guests or interviews.
13. Is attractive to the social networks.
14. Has a long tail.

FAQ 45. Is there an objective way to determine good content?

Indeed providing good content is a necessary part of any blogger's strategy to be recognized by the search engines.

On or near the top of the list for good content is writing something that is unique.

This might be hard considering Solomon's insight, "There is nothing new under the sun."

But I don't think it's that hard especially if it comes from you, in your voice, at this point in your life with everything else that is going on around you.

I already mentioned voice in a previous post. The gist of that post is if you are not you, then who will be you?

Providing unique content is all about putting something up on the web that nobody else has.

Robobloggers and their ilk are smothering the blogosphere. Thankfully, search engines are recognizing duplicate content and burying it at the bottom of the pile or putting it on news pages worthy of lining the bottom of bird cages.

Unique content is fresh and different and search engines respond with "Wow, I have never seen anything like this before" by placing your content in a meaningful place in the rankings.

Write something that hasn't been written before, or at least in a way that only you know how to say it, and you are on your way to good content.

Churning out good, unique content is fundamental when blogging for money.

FAQ 46. How important is it to consider the reader when blogging?

Blogging for Money tip 43, good content strategy 2 is about writing something people want to know about.

That's not as obvious as some might think.

Lots of writers want to tell people what they know, not tell people what they (the readers) want to know.

It's different.

When you write for yourself and don't particularly care if people read your stuff or not, it doesn't really matter what you write.

However, if you want to get read, you will consider what people might have an interest in and write about that.

Election season? Holiday coming up? Anniversary of some big event? Breaking news? Big sporting event? Everyone looking for a recipe to do the same thing?

Write about what you know about what people want to know about. Wow! That's a lot of *abouts* in one sentence.

Don't just write about what you think is interesting, write about what you think other people will think is interesting.

FAQ 47. How important is it for the blogger to provide something fresh?

At some point there really isn't much more that can be said about a topic.

Opinions are a lot like excuses and my dad says excuses are like rear ends (he referred to a more specific location), everyone has one and they all stink.

Adding to the discussion is about giving the blogosphere something new, something nobody else has heard, a new perspective, a different insight.

And when you have nothing else to add, how about

1. Trying to make sense of everything has been said?
2. Ranking the Top Five most interesting comments on the topic of the day?
3. Linking all the interesting stuff that is being said into one post?
4. Disagreeing just for the fun of it, or to create a discussion?
5. Providing links to maps of where events took place?
6. Providing links to more info about characters involved in the topic you are discussing?
7. Dissing your own opinion and going after a historical figure's opinion?

Make a contribution or be quiet. The blogosphere is already crowded.

FAQ 48. How can a blogger predict something that will be timely?

Do a search—On This Day. Type in a day that's coming up and you'll have a bit of an idea of what people might be thinking about when that day rolls around.

On December 17th Orville and Wilbur Wright made the first successful man-powered airplane flight, near Kitty Hawk, N.C. Now had I fixed something about those guys in my title and applied them to blogging for money, chances are this post would have been found a bit more by the search engines.

Wilbur Wright publishes plans for man-powered flight on his blog, makes six figures—or something like that.

What does your topic have to do with what is going on right now? Or with what people will be thinking about in the coming days?

If you can make that connection from time to time (hence, timely), your blog will get more traffic.

FAQ 49. How can a blogger attract repeat traffic?

In theory, this blog post being part of a series is a post that will encourage the reader to come back and follow along in the series. Maybe even the reader will go back and read previous posts in the series. Whichever or both, I am trying to encourage the reader to come back.

Interviews work.

Guest bloggers work.

Hosting a poll works.

Link of the day.

Link of the week.

Review of the day/week.

A contest works.

Starting a fight works. What I mean, of course, is having a post that attracts enough comments and discussion that readers come back to see who else is saying what else about the topic at hand.

Making a promise at the end of a post of an upcoming and attractive topic in a subsequent post works also.

FAQ 50. How can bloggers solicit comments to their blog?

Comments are important because each time someone leaves a comment at your post it changes the post, meaning the search engines will have to come back to find out why.

Enough legitimate comments at a post will cause that post to climb the page rankings.

So, what's the best way to get comments at a post?

I am glad that I am sitting behind a computer screen far away from you, the reader, in distance and time (this post will go on December 20 and I am writing it on November 9), but the best way I have found to get comments to a post is to ask a question.

Stick a "What do you think?" at the end of the post.

Or a "Do you agree?"

Or, if you are up for it, pick a fight about your topic. Play the devil's advocate.

Go to another blog that is related to your topic and find someone who doesn't agree with your position and leave a comment there with a link back to the post where you wrote your contrary position. Perhaps that will lure them and the readers there to your site.

Or you might just ask:

What is the best way you have found to get people to leave a comment at your site?

And see if anybody responds.

FAQ 51. How can bloggers write something that will go viral?

I don't know what the definition of *viral* is in terms of number of hits. If several thousand people visit one of your posts, is that good?

How about 10,000?

Or 50,000?

I looked the other day at my Google Analytics account. I didn't install it until early 2009, some 3 years after I started my blogs so the numbers are not complete.

Even so, I have 260 posts that have received more than 10,000 page views.

I have more than a dozen that have gone over 100,000 page views.

I have four posts that went over 200,000 page views.

Are those viral numbers?

So, what did I do to make those numbers happen?

The simple and honest answer: nothing. Just wrote regular stuff on a consistent basis and some of them caught on.

I have learned the answer to the question, "What will the next hot topic online be?"

The answer: nobody knows.

Granted there are groups on Digg and Stumbleupon and the like that will vote on a post until it catches on. Think the herd mentality.

Then thousands and tens of thousands of people might show up to your post. But that kind of traffic does NOT earn good money. Why bother?

If your goal is to make money blogging, trying to write the next hot topic will not help. You are better off writing good consistent stuff day in and day out.

Thomas Jefferson said, "I have learned that the harder I work the luckier I am" or words to that effect.

Work hard and luck will follow your blog and traffic, the good kind, will come, the kind that makes money.

FAQ 52. What is a pillar post?

A pillar post, also known as an evergreen post, is the kind of post that can be and is searched for a long time.

Here are a few examples of posts I wrote at PanAsianBiz a long, long time ago.

20 Must-Know Facts about Gaza Strip + Map

21 Must Know Facts about India + Map

20 Facts about the Great Wall of China – And One Myth Debunked ...

They still get traffic, have seen over 10,000 page views each, and will get traffic for a long time to come.

These are pillar posts. (I have a lot more similar to them.)

Every blogger should be writing such posts for his or her site on a regular basis.

For what it's worth, these are the kinds of posts that can catch on.

They are also the kind of post that people like to link to and include at their sites. If you wrote them with the intention of getting links they may be called linkbait posts. I just wrote them because I thought my readers would appreciate them.

And, I had fun writing them as well!

FAQ 53. How important is a long tail to bloggers?

I want to make mention of the long tail.

A post will usually get as much traffic (more) as it does after the first bit of traffic it gets.

If a post gets found and passed around by social media, there is an initial surge. The long tail means the amount of traffic that will come in subsequent days will exceed the initial surge.

A blogger will want to write posts that have initial appeal. And when/if it does, the blogger can count on that post to get at least that much traffic or more over the long term.

This kind of post is golden, good for traffic numbers and good for income.

Write good stuff, expect it to be found, and anticipate readers for the long run.

GLOSSARY

A

A Penny A Page—video introduction of Bill Belew created by a team of Google (yeah, that Google) videographers.
adwords—words sold by search engines with a promise to have them appear in search engine results.
algorithms—a funky formula created by search engines to keep people guessing about how they (the search engines) decide what to display when real people do searches.
audience—your readers.

B

backlinks—links coming to your site from other websites. Also known as trackbacks.
blog—web log. A running account of things you write about in reverse chronological order.
blogger—a dude or dudette who sits at home in their pajamas munching on cereal and chips all day long ... not. Okay, well sometimes. But not me.
blogosphere—70 million some blogs trying to find each other and be found on the Web.
BlogWorldExpo—where serious bloggers gather once a year to learn, network, and take their blogging to a higher level.
bookmark—using your browser to set pages you want to come back to without searching.
bounce rate—the percentage of visitors who come to your site, then leave because they didn't like what they found.
branding—giving people an image of how you want to be thought of.
business blog—using a blog to get business done. Think inbound and content marketing.

C

caption—those few words you can see underneath an image that allow the image to be searchable.
comment spam—commenters put the same comment all over the place hoping somebody will approve the comment and generate a backlink.
content marketing—creating high-quality blog material that is business related and findable.
convert—getting what you want from your visitors—email, contact info, phone call, purchase.
cyberspace—where magic happens.

D

dashboard—where you go to publish and work on your blog.
direct mail—emails to people who have asked you to contact them.
direct traffic—when people open up their laptop, PC, or mobile device, and type in your domain name.

E

external link—connecting to other credible sites in your niche.

F

feedback—good, bad and ugly but insightful enough to help you improve.
freebie blog—WordPress.com, blogspot, tumblr—setting up a lemonade stand in somebody else's front yard.

G

googlebot—search spider that comes to see what is happening at your site.

H

hit—a visit to your web server. Hits are many times more than visits and mean nothing. You want people to read the page not just whack it with a hammer.

I

inbound marketing—creating content that is attractive to clients and converts into sales.
incoming traffic—visitors coming to your site.
information marketer—a guy or gal who makes money selling know-how.
interactive capability—the *social* in social media. Going back and forth with your commenters on your site in response to something you wrote.
internal blog—networks have internal blogs where only bloggers within the network can hang out and write stuff for each other.
internal link—connecting to yourself within your own site. Showing your readers and searchbots that you are on topic here, there and there, and ...
interval—how often your posts go out.

K

keyword specific—on topic.

L

legitimate traffic—not pushed traffic. Not driving traffic. Visitors coming to your site because they really, I mean *really,* want to be there.
long tail—content that lasts long after it was first read.

M

metrics—measuring the effectiveness of your site with numbers. People who say numbers don't matter, usually don't have any numbers.
mini-network—a small (relative term) of like-minded and somewhat related niche group of bloggers.
monetize—making money from your site.

N

network—you and him and her and all of them connected by relevance of topic or niche.
New Media Live—BlogWorldExpo.
newsfeed—when the news alerts show up in your email box.
niche—your focus, your topic. What makes your heart go pitter patter.

O

online advertiser—images and links on your website that want click-throughs so they can sell something.

organic growth—more people coming to your site just because you write more good stuff and more people are coming online who are interested in your topic.

outbound marketing—going to networking events, buying adwords, working the social networks, emailing, wearing sandwich boards, ...

P

pillar post—a post that is well written and read for a very long time. Enough of these will hold up your site = pillar.

problogger—the guy or gal who pays their bills with their blog.

R

ratio—the number of page views compared to the number of unique visitors. The higher the better.

referral traffic—when another site or social network sends visitors to your site via a link.

related links—other pages/posts within your site that are on topic with the subject of the current post.

residual traffic—keeps on coming long after the post was first read

revenue—money from your content.

S

screen shot—a picture or image of what your PC is showing.

search engine—Google, Yahoo, Bing, Dogpile, Blekko, ...

search engine optimization—good content that is appealing to real people and to search engines, in that order.

search traffic—visitors coming to your site because they put something in a search box and found you.

searchbot—a search engine spider that is crawling around your site to see what is happening, how often it is happening and counting words and calculating percentages to determine the focus.

sitemeter—a free way to see who is coming to your site.

social media—publishing that is interactive with readers and writers. Blogs are king.

social media strategy—using your blog to interact with your readers for a desired end result.

social network—Facebook, Google+, Twitter, LinkedIn, and the like. People hanging out under pretenses of getting something from someone else—a referral, a tip, an insight, business

spam prevention—keeping the spammers off your site. Akismet. Captchas...

subscriber—when visitors voluntarily give you their email so that whenever you hit the publish button to your blog the post shows up in their email box.

T

tagline—the focus of your blog in ten words or less—no adjectives, adverbs, conjunctions, articles, or prepositions.

tradeshow—where people of like interests gather to peddle their stuff. Great place for bloggers to hang out and offer to write for pay.

typo—hitting the wrong key. It is different from not knowing how to spell.

U

unique visitor—somebody who hasn't been to your website before.
URL—uniform resource locator. I had to look it up, too.

V

viral—when something you write gets caught by a reader and they pass it on to someone else who passes it on to someone else who ....

W

web hosting service—BM2hosting, GoDaddy, JustHost... a little dark, somewhat cool room in AZ where your blog content lives.
well-trafficked—totally relative number, but more people coming to your site than your competitor's site.
widget—what you slide around via your dashboard at your WordPress blog that lets your blog do things—add a calendar, put in an ad, connect to social networks. If you can imagine you want to do it, somebody has created a widget that will do it.
WordPress—hands down the best content management system for bloggers. Kind of like a sophisticated email client but better. If WordPress can't do it, your website doesn't need it.
WordPress nerd—little boys and girls (I am old so that's a relative term) that hang out at Wordcamps and in WordPress Meetups that can help you do things with your WordPress blog.